ONE HUNDRED HILL WALKS AROUND GLASGOW

ONE HUNDRED HILL WALKS AROUND GLASGOW

JOHN CHALMERS

MAINSTREAM PUBLISHING

3rd Edition 1993
2nd Edition 1990
Reprinted 1994

First published in Great Britain in 1988 by
MAINSTREAM PUBLISHING COMPANY
(EDINBURGH) LTD
7 Albany Street
Edinburgh EH1 3UG

ISBN 1 85158 538 9

A catalogue record for this book is available from the British
Library.

Typeset in 11/12pt Times by Pulse Origination and Bookworm
Typesetting, Edinburgh.
Printed and bound in Great Britain by The Cromwell Press,
Broughton Gifford, Melksham.

The sketch maps are by the author. The photographs on pages
23, 107, 111, 113, 137 and 159 are by Donald Bennett; on
pages 27, 37 and 181 by L. S. Paterson, and on pages 26, 62,
63, 89 and 91 by the author.

CONTENTS

ABOUT THIS BOOK

Those who live in Glasgow have the great fortune to have hills all around them upon which they can walk and enjoy a healthy recreation with unending variety. The tradition of open access for careful and considerate walkers is well entrenched. I know of no other city which is so well endowed.

To help and encourage those who live in Greater Glasgow to go upon the hills this book gives details of 100 walks each of which can be completed in one day, using a car to get to the starting point. It is a practical guide to be used in planning the walks and when on the hills. It enables the readers to choose between far and near from home, and between short and long distances on foot. It also allows a choice between high climbs and not-so-high climbs. It tells how to shorten each walk should this become necessary. Remember that hill walking is for all ages. I learned when I was a boy and I am now a septuagenarian.

One of the appeals of hill walking is the solitude — the getting away from the bustle of town life. Many of the walks described ensure this by giving routes which are not walked often, which have no paths or signposts, but are attractive just because of that. Hill walkers will quickly devise variations of their own making, to develop their urge for exploration, their need for isolation, and their desire for achievement.

Names such as the Campsie Fells, Kilpatrick Hills, Gleniffer Braes, Cathkin Braes tell us of the hills we see from our doorstep. Then we look farther afield to Fintry, Gargunnock and Touch Hills, the mountains of the Trossachs and around Loch Lomond and Loch Long, the Ochil Hills and those in Clydesdale and bordering the regions of Dumfries and Galloway, Lothian, and the Borders. Nor do we forget the local hills in Cunninghame, Renfrew and Inverclyde and many more. All these areas are covered in this book which the author hopes will satisfy its readers.

So, go ahead and enjoy the hills around you!

ACKNOWLEDGEMENTS

To my late father must be directed my first acknowledgement since it was he who introduced me to the wonder of the hills at an early age. To all those clubs and groups with whom I rambled over the years I also owe a debt. For help in preparing this book I wish to thank Reg Currie with whom I walked over most of the routes and who checked over some of the manuscripts; and my old friend and hillwalker Jim Hunter who willingly and generously gave practical assistance and advice on many of the technicalities. To my son, Colin, for assistance in connection with the sketch maps. For companionship on the walks I do not forget Joe Bell, Archie Chalmers, Arthur Craig, Jim Donaldson, Bill Frame, David and Mary Spence, Lex Watson and Fred Wylie. Of my wife, Anne, I ask forgiveness for neglecting her to spend hours preparing the book when I should have been giving her my attention, and I record my thanks to her for encouraging me to go ahead with its preparation.

ABOUT THE THIRD EDITION

Because of its success, once again it has been necessary to issue a new edition to meet the demands of an ever growing number of hill walkers. And again a number of changes, some resulting from readers' letters, have been introduced to bring it up-to-date so far as that is possible. Could I make a plea to hill walkers using the book to continue to act with responsibility when on the hills, as by doing so they help to prevent restrictions on future walkers.

ABBREVIATIONS

km	kilometres.
ml	miles.
m	metres.
f	feet.
y	yards.
NN-, NS-, NT-, NX-	The National Grid reference.
N, S, E, W	The directions of the compass.
(- m - f)	Metres and feet above sea level — no triangulation pillar.
(- m - f TP)	Metres and feet above sea level — with a triangulation pillar.
BM -	Bench mark — the flush bracket serial number as shown on triangulation pillar.
M -, A -, B -	Road numbers.
Munro	Any mountain in Scotland 3000 feet or more in height. Named after Sir Hugh T. Munro, Bart.
Corbett	Any mountain in Scotland 2500 feet to 2999 feet in height. Named after Mr J. Rooke Corbett.

GAELIC AND SCOTS WORDS

Words	Pronounced	Meaning
a', an	ah, ahn	the, this (often used before names of places).
allt	alt	a burn, a river.
beag	bake	little, small.
bealach	by alach	a pass, or lowest point, between hills.
beinn	bane	a mountain.
bin	bin	a hill (a form of 'ben').
carn	karn	a cairn, a rocky hill.
col	cawl	a gap between two mountains, a bealach.
corrie	cawri	a hollow in a hillside.
creag	kragg	a crag, a rock.
cruach	croo-ach	a stack
cruachan	croo-a-han	a conical hill.
dod	dawd	a bare hill with a rounded top.
dubh, dhubh	doo (short)	black, dark.
dun	doon (long)	a hillock, a fort.
fell	fel	a rocky hill.
garbh, gharbh	garv	rough, rugged, thick.
knowe	now	a knoll
lane	lain	a waterway between two lochs.
law	law	a rounded hill, usually isolated.
maol	may ol	a bare top.
meall	myall	a rounded hill.
meikle	meekle	large.
mor, mhor	mo-ar	great, big.
muir	moor	an alternative spelling of 'moor'.
rig	rig	a ridge.
sgorr	skawr	a rocky, pointed hill.
squrr	skoor	a rocky, pointed hill.
spout	spowt	a waterfall, especially coming from a cleft in rocks or a spring.
sron	srawn	a peak, a spur.
stuc	stoog	a steep, rocky peak.
tumulus	toomyoolus	a heap of earth covering prehistoric tomb (also called a 'barrow' and 'chambered cairn').

SYMBOLS ON SKETCH MAPS

P   Parking place and start of walk.

⟶   Route of walk.

⟶≫   Up hill.

▭   Building.

———   Fence or wall.

 Woodland.

 Water.

O   Hill top.

∩∩∩   Rocky face of hill.

⋀   Overhead electric power line.

⸸   Television or radar mast.

 Archaeological site.

—+—+—   Railway.

NOTES

1. The sketch maps are to give a quick visual idea of each walk. They are not to scale. They do not replace the Ordnance Survey maps, the appropriate sheet of which should always be carried. These maps are the 1:50,000 Landranger Series. Since three of the sheets, 56, 57 and 64, cover sixty-three of the walks in the book there is no need to buy all the sheets to start.

2. The 'Distance from city centre to car parking' is as it says, but remember it is also the same distance back, so have petrol in the tank for double the distance stated.

3. The 'Walking distance from parking' includes an allowance for the continuous variations from the route as it would be measured on the map. It is always necessary on a hill walk to make short detours to avoid bog, rocks, hillocks, etc. While an allowance has been made for this, the resultant figure must be approximate.

4. The 'Height of climbing' is calculated, in a walk where there are 'ups-and-downs', by adding all the 'ups' together. Many hill walks involve descending some way from one top before climbing another. So it is the height of all the upward climbing which makes this figure.

5. Conditions in the countryside change; new forests are planted, fences are erected, new roads are laid over agricultural land, etc. So you may find variations from what is written in the text, but these should not prevent you from finding a way round them. While every endeavour has been made to be accurate in all details, should some errors have crept in I apologise for these in advance. No responsibility can be accepted for any loss, etc. caused by an inaccuracy; and the fact that a walk is described in this book does not infer a right of way nor does it guarantee that access will always be available.

6. If any reader should point out that the walks round Loch Chon (26) and over Flanders Moss (21) are not up or on the hills, let him think of the high mountains surrounding the former and those within sight both north and south of the latter; and realise that there are days when even the most keen hill walker wants to take it easy without losing touch.

THE WALKS

As indicated on page 11 the Walks described are not necessarily Rights of Way, but established routes are followed wherever possible. The attention of readers is also drawn to the section on page 233 regarding rights and responsibilities, and it is hoped that users of this book will take every care to avoid doing damage while following the routes, and so maintain and improve the good relationship that exists between walker and land-owner in Scotland. It has been particularly requested by sheep farmers that when they ask walkers to leave their land that they do so without argument.

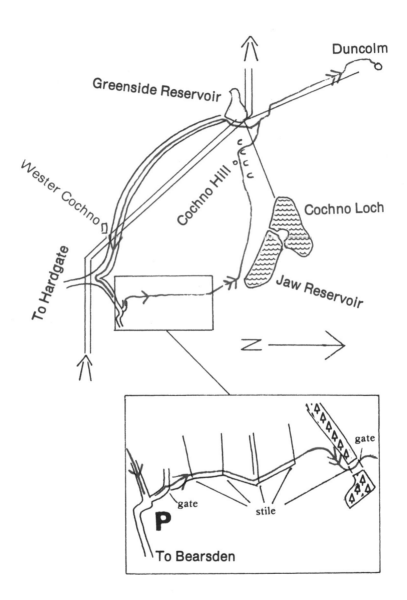

WALK 1

KILPATRICK HILLS

1. Cochno Loch, Duncolm and Greenside Reservoir.

Ordnance Survey map 64. Distance from city centre to car parking: 10.3km 6.4ml. Walking distance from parking: 17.2km 10.7ml. Height of climbing: 328m 1076 f. Easy and pleasant walking with gentle climbing. Good views over the Clyde basin. The name 'Cochno' means 'place of little cups' and refers to cup and ring markings on stone in the area.

Park car in space at side of road near E entrance to Cochno estate (Glasgow University Agricultural Department). NS503740. To get there take A81 or A739 to Bearsden, then A810 towards Hardgate. Turn right up minor road just past extensive overhead electricity distribution network. Follow round this road to entrance marked 'Cochno Farm. Private'. Park here.

Enter Cochno Farm road and walk along for about 100m 110y. On coming out of the woodland turn right over a gate and onto a wayleave and pipe track (granted at one time as access for anglers to the hill lochs). Continue alongside wood until first stile. Cross this and follow along fence on right. Go over second stile and along farm track, then over third stile at side of gate. Proceed along farm track which becomes path, over fourth stile at gate. Make for woodland. Turn uphill with woodland on your left. At the top cross remnants of fifth stile, then through a gate and follow a path to right up a hill. (At the left side of the early part of this path is a spring, which can be overgrown. Help to clear it if you have the time. It provides a welcome, cool drink on a hot

15

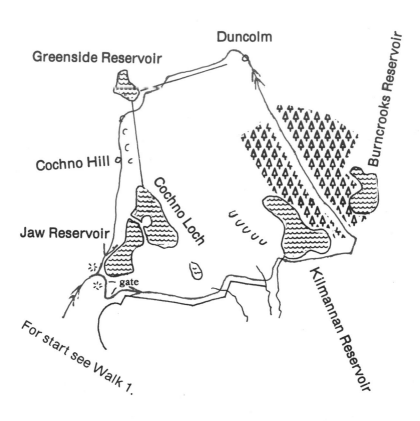

WALK 2

day.) Soon you will be at the Jaw Reservoir. Turn slightly left uphill, alongside the Jaw but at a higher level than the waterside path (which can be dangerous). Keep along above Cochno Loch to Cochno Hill (347m. 1138f. Small cairn). Then turn right down to break in the dyke which comes from Cochno Loch (and goes to Greenside Reservoir). Now cross up and over tufty ground slightly left, through a col, and up to a dyke coming from Duncolm (and goes to Greenside Reservoir). Cross dyke in order to get a better path up beside it, and follow this. Just before the dyke starts to rise more steeply, follow a path to the left which leads you up to left shoulder and avoids a rocky approach to the summit of Duncolm (401m 1314f. TP. BM 3666).

Return S alongside dyke, but continue to Greenside Reservoir, going round E side to road at dam. Follow this down, passing Wester Cochno farm (empty), to minor road. Turn left and back to car.

To shorten the walk, after Cochno Hill walk to Greenside Reservoir (omitting Duncolm). Save 7km 4.4ml.

2. Cochno Loch and Kilmannan Reservoir.

Ordnance Survey map 64. Distance from city centre to car parking: 10.3km 6.4ml. Walking distance from parking 20.9km 13ml. Height of climbing: 368m 1207f. An interesting variation of previous walk in the Kilpatrick Hills, and rather longer.

Park car near Cochno estate. NS503740. See walk 1.

Walk until start of Jaw Reservoir (see walk 1). Note two mounds of earth (covering prehistoric tombs — shown on map as 'Maiden Paps'). Turn right along dam of reservoir and continue on track. Go through gate on wall on right, then continue on track on other side of wall. When wall turns left, follow track beside it. Go through gate and continue on track turning right. Then strike over marshy ground on left and up to fence round forestry. Go left and then when fence turns at right angles, follow it. Shortly there is a wall on your right.

17

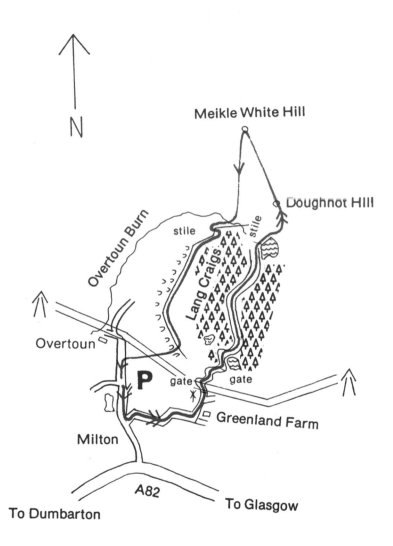

Meikle White Hill

Doughnot Hill

Overtoun Burn

stile

stile

Lang Craigs

Overtoun

P

gate

gate

Greenland Farm

Milton

A82

To Dumbarton

To Glasgow

N

WALK 3

Follow this. Latterly, it turns sharp left. Continue following it. It comes to a stream and is continued on other side, turning left. Don't cross stream. Follow along to left and soon you will be at Kilmannan Reservoir (also known as 'The Baker') and a waterworks road. Here you cross from Strathclyde to Central Region for a short spell. Follow this until Burncrooks Reservoir appears, then turn left along a firebreak which goes all the way through the forest to the foot of Duncolm (401m 1314f. TP. BM 3666). From Duncolm go SE following dyke, but before it reaches Greenside Reservoir turn left at an angle and go through a gap in a wall. Then climb through a col up to Cochno Loch to end of Jaw Reservoir, and so to start.

To shorten the walk, return from Kilmannan Reservoir by outward route. Save 9km 5.6ml.

3.   Doughnot Hill, Meikle White Hill and Lang Craigs.

Ordnance Survey map 64. Distance from city centre to car parking: 19.8km 12.3ml. Walking distance from parking: 14.2km 8.8ml. Height of climbing: 368m 1207f. This walk on the western Kilpatrick Hills is pleasant and easy. The view from the tops over the Clyde and Loch Lomond to the mountains beyond is surprisingly good.

Park car at top of Milton Brae Road at entrance to Overtoun. NS426756. To get there, take A82 (Glasgow to Dumbarton) but turn right at Milton, which is past Bowling and near where the road turns left at an angle beside a filling station.

Walk back along road, then turn up road going off on the E (not the first, nor the second to Middleton) and continue to and pass Greenland farm. Past quarry entrance on right and television mast on left. Go through gate. The road zig-zags here, over a ford, and under overhead electric line, before rising to another gate at entrance to forestry. The road again twists round a small reservoir on the right. When you come out of the trees on the right there is Black Linn Reservoir. Walk to its

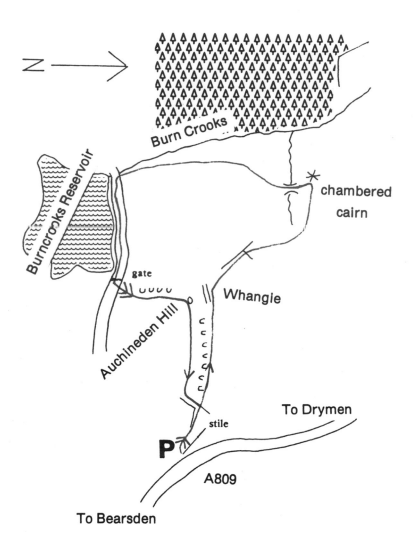

WALK 4

end, go over stile, and along top of dam. A path from here leads up to ridge from Brown Hill, but you turn with it along to summit of Doughnot Hill (374m 1227f. TP. BM S5142).

Then go NNW to Meikle White Hill (354m 1162f). Return along W side of Doughnot Hill and descend to and cross burn near forest. Climb up along path to old road, turn left along it and go over stile. Turn right and walk up hill between old fence and forest. This starts you on a longish path walk along the top of the sheer rock face of Lang Craigs. For safety, keep on the hill side of the fence. Ultimately the path turns through the fence and descends steeply (but quite safely) to near the driveway at Overtoun House. A break in the wall allows you on to this. Turn left and back to car.

To shorten the walk, omit Meikle White Hill. Save 2.6km 1.6ml.

4. The Whangie and Burncrooks Reservoir

Ordnance Survey map 64. Distance from city centre to car parking: 18km 11.2ml. Walking distance from parking: 13.1km 8.2ml. Height of climbing: 240m 787f. A popular walk to the Whangie which is a fascinating sight, followed by a varied walk on moor, by reservoir and burn, and over heather.

Park car at Queen's View car park at start of Stockie Muir on A809 (Bearsden to Drymen). NS512808. To get there take A81 to Canniesburn then through Bearsden, turning right with A809.

Crossing dyke by stile, follow path up and along hillside, crossing ladder stile on the way. If you are observant and not too low, you will see the Little Whangie on the way. While not losing height, do not take path leading to top of hill. Reach the Whangie. This spectacular natural phenomenon — a rock face cleft in two — is worth exploring. It is 15m 50f deep, and 93m 300f long, and was probably caused by the retreating ice at the end of the ice age. A more interesting explanation is that the devil had been holding a meeting of his favourite witches and warlocks on the Campsie Fells. He had another gathering to attend at Dumbarton. On his way, in a jovial mood, he whisked his tail which struck the shoulder of Auchineden Hill, shearing through the rock — and so the Whangie was the result.

Just before reaching the Whangie, there is a faint path leading down (WNW). Go down this, and round small hillock. Follow beside fence on left until another fence meets it from the right. Cross the latter, and head at an angle to the right down to the right side of the burn. Follow this to and past a small bridge over it (this carries water pipe from Burncrooks Reservoir). The ruins of a chambered cairn can soon be seen on your right. This cairn is thought to be 2000-3000 years old.

After examining the cairn, retrace your steps to the small bridge. Cross this and follow path. It becomes indistinct, but keep to the bottom of the ploughed-up area until it ends. Then turn up to meet the path to the right. Follow this down to dam of Burncrooks Reservoir.

Turn left along reservoir road. When past gate with stile at side look for hill ridge on left with a path going up it. Go over and up the path. It leads along the top of a precipitous rock face on the left, but with plenty of room on the right. When near the top, cross over to the second ridge on the right. Another path goes along its edge to the left. Follow this. Look for pillar and walk to summit of Auchineden Hill (357m 1171f TP. BM 3638).

Follow path going E, past a cairn. At a division of the path, go right. This will take you to a small plantation, and steeply down to ladder stile near beginning of your walk. And so to car.

To reduce climbing, from Burncrooks Reservoir continue on road, instead of going up Auchineden Hill, until joining A809 then turn left back to car. Save a climb of 91m 300f, but add 1.6km 1ml.

Dumgoyne. Walk 7.

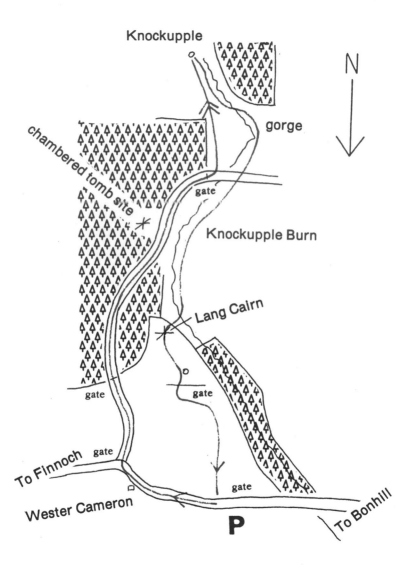

Knockupple

gorge

N

chambered tomb site

gate

Knockupple Burn

Lang Cairn

gate

gate

To Finnoch   gate

Wester Cameron

gate

P

To Bonhill

WALK   5

5. *Knockupple*

Ordnance Survey map 64. Distance from city centre to car parking: 33.3km 20.7ml. Walking distance from parking: 15.8km 9.8ml. Height of climbing: 257m 843f. A pleasant walk through forest to hill top, with the added attraction of a chambered cairn.

Park car on road between Gallangad road end and Wester Cameron farm. NS450831. To get there, go by A82 (Glasgow to Balloch) but at roundabout at NE outskirts of Dumbarton follow road for Bonhill. Just before small housing estate in Bonhill turn right along road marked 'Auchincarroch Road', and proceed 6.6km 4.1 ml, latterly going along the part marked 'No through road'.

Walk 1.3km 0.8ml along road to forestry road on right. This has a gate at its entrance, but it is not signposted nor has any trees at its start. Go along this road. At the start of the forest there is another gate. Walk quite a way along this road. Near the highest point (230m 755f) on the left note a small cairn about 50m 55y off the road, with various large stones lying around. This is the site of the Shiels of Gartlea chambered tomb. Four stones of the façade survive, together with the remains of an axial chamber behind them.

Continue on forestry road until shortly after it emerges from forest at a gate. Leave road and walk up rough path on left side of burn beside forest. At top of forest climb to Knockupple summit (341m 1118f).

Descend W and skirt round woodland and beside Knockupple Burn. There is a deep gorge here, but the burn can be crossed near the woodland. Follow down the left side of burn crossing road, and continue until end of forest on right. Cross burn then fence, turn right into field on right, when the chambered tomb, known as 'The Lang Cairn', can be seen. The age is variously put at Neolithic (4000-2400BC), 1800BC, and Bronze Age (2000-500BC). Below the N side there are remains of old road over which limestone was carried.

Go NNW over marshy ground to top (170m 558f. TP.

BM S4987). Go through gate to farm road and follow this down to road with car.

To shorten the walk, on emerging from forest turn right along return route (omitting the climb up Knockupple). Save 4.4km 2.8ml.

Duncolm. Walks 1 and 2.

Ben Lomond. Walk 39.

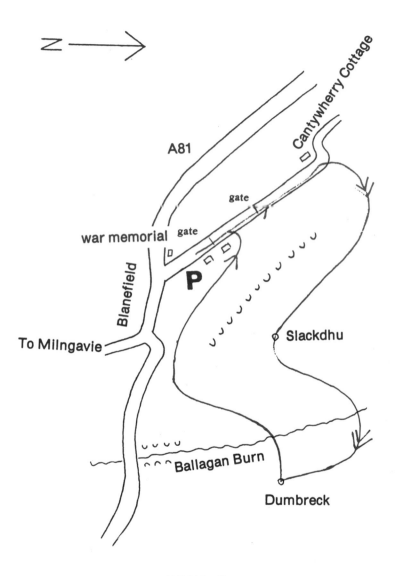

WALK 6

CAMPSIE FELLS—
STRATHBLANE HILLS

6. Slackdhu and Dumbreck.

Ordnance Survey map 64. Distance from city centre to car parking: 18.7km 11.6ml. Walking distance from parking: 11.7km 7.3ml. Height of climbing: 513m 1683f. One of the nearest hill walks for most Glaswegians. Heathery, peaty, and with numerous sheep tracks. Wide open spaces.

Park car along Campsie Dene road. NS553803. To get there take A81 (via Canniesburn) to Blanefield, and turn off to right at war memorial. If there are many cars parked in this private road, it is recommended that a transfer be made to Walk 8 or Walk 12.

Walk along this road (which is really the pipe track for Glasgow's water supply from Loch Katrine). There may be some locked gates to be climbed over. Shortly before Cantywherry Cottage, leave the road, turning right onto the hills. Make for the end of the ridge in a NE direction, climb this, and when on top, go SE to top of Slackdhu (495m 1624f). Pause here to look at the view over the city to the S. Then walk NE to enable you to cross the Ballagan Burn more easily, going on to Owsen Hill, then SSE to Dumbreck (508m 1665f. TP. BM 3669). Dumbreck is on the boundary between Strathclyde and Central Regions, and probably few realise that the former is to the E and the latter to the W.

On leaving Dumbreck drop into the valley of, and

29

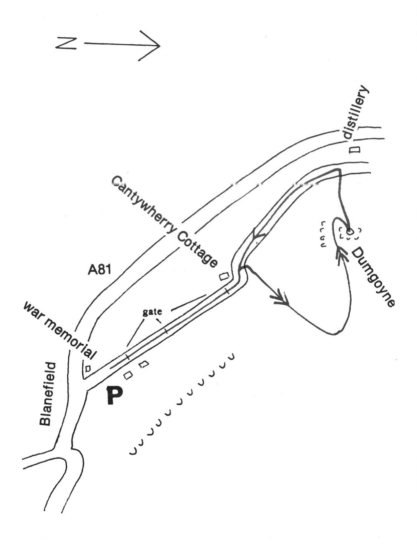

N →

distillery

Cantywherry Cottage

A81

Dumgoyne

war memorial

gate

Blanefield

P

WALK 7

crossing, Ballagan Burn and go S alongside it until the precipitous part in which is the Spout of Ballagan. (On another occasion you might wish to visit the Spout from the S and see the revealed strata of such great interest to geologists.) Strike W along the lower side of the hills (not too low at first since it can be boggy) until you can join the pipe track road just past some woodlands and houses. Then back to the car.

To shorten the walk, return from Slackdhu by outward route. Save 4km 2.5ml.

7. Dumgoyne

Ordnance Survey maps 57 or 64. Distance from city centre to car parking: 18.7km 11.6ml. Walking distance from parking: 12.1km 7.5ml. Height of climbing: 320m 1050f. Quite a low hill, but a landmark giving a grand view.

Park car along Campsie Dene road. NS553803. To get there take A81 (via Canniesburn) to Blanefield, then turn off to right at war memorial. If there are many cars parked in this private road, it is recommended that a transfer be made to Walk 8 or Walk 12.

Walk along this road, perhaps having to climb over some locked gates. Immediately past Cantywherry Cottage the road goes over two bridges. Just before the second, turn right onto hills through gate. Follow track up side of burn. Higher up it crosses burn and through a wall, continuing along foot of unnamed hill before ascending to N end of Dumgoyne. Turn right up to top (427m 1402f). There is no pillar or cairn at the summit — only a few stones. To return, descend at N end and drop down in the direction of the Dumgoyne distillery, easily to be seen in clear weather, until the pipe line road is reached, where turn left and back to start. When returning from the top, care should be taken as there are some vertical faces.

To shorten the walk, return from Dumgoyne summit by outward route. Save 3.1km 1.9ml.

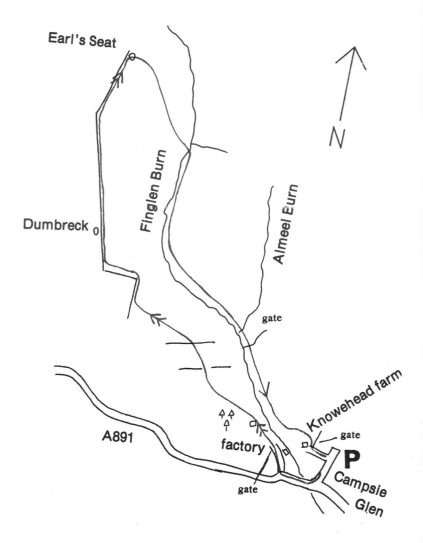

Earl's Seat

Dumbreck

Finglen Burn

Almeel Eurn

gate

A891

factory

gate

Knowehead farm

gate

P

Campsie
Glen

WALK 8

8. Earl's Seat and Fin Glen.

Ordnance Survey map 57 or 64. Distance from city centre to car parking: 18.7km 11.6ml. Walking distance from parking: 20km 12.4ml. Height of climbing: 550m 1804f. A most interesting and varied walk, though quite long. Not to be undertaken in misty weather.

Park car at Campsie Glen. NS610796. To get there proceed via Bishopbriggs, Torrance and Lennoxtown. Continue on A891, turning off along road marked 'Clachan of Campsie'.

Walk back to A891, turn right, after 0.5km 0.3ml turn right along road marked 'Morris of Glasgow'. After passing the factory, proceed along farm road, through right gate, over rising field, to right side of ruined farm buildings. Then follow track towards right end of trees on hill, keeping Finglen Burn in sight on right. Note the waterfalls, called the Black Spout and, higher, the White Spout. When past woodlands, make for ridge of the hill, through gap in first dyke, then climb over second dyke. Keep up to wire fence and follow it (it has two opposite right hand turns) up to Dumbreck (508m 1665f. TP. BM 3669). Then go N, still following fence, which is on the Strathclyde/Central Regions boundary, avoiding some peat bog on the way by diverging slightly left, and so to Earl's Seat (578m 1896f. TP. BM S1622), the highest hill in the Campsies.

Return by walking SE to cross Finglen Burn. Follow the burn, keeping just below the top of the hill. Use sheep paths where evident. After a deep gully, an old road track starts at a gate. This leads along hillside to Knowehead farm. Avoid going through the farm by cutting across and down field to gate in dyke. Go through gate and sharply down to road from farm. This leads down to Campsie Glen.

To shorten the walk, return from Dumbreck by outward route. Save 6km 3.7ml.

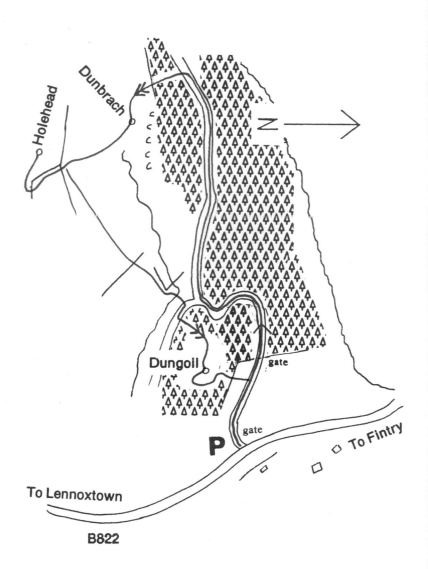

Holehead

Dunbrach

N →

Dungoil

gate

gate

P

To Lennoxtown

To Fintry

B822

WALK   9

9. *Holehead and Dungoil.*

Ordnance Survey map 57. Distance from city centre to car parking: 26.2km 16.3ml. Walking distance from parking: 14.2km 8.8ml. Height of climbing: 427m 1401f. An easy walk on a quiet part of the Campsies.

Park car on B822 (Lennoxtown to Fintry — the Crow Road) as near NS640852 as possible. To get there, proceed via Bishopbriggs, Torrance and Lennoxtown. On your way over the Crow Road you pass a building which was the Campsiemuir Tollhouse used in the 18th century on what was then a drove road. Well down the other side look for a hut on the right above a dyke. On the road, opposite this, is a gate on the left which is the entrance to hill road to forestry. Park here without blocking entrance, or motor back up road to first parking place.

Go through gate and up road. This winds up below forestry and Dungoil. It then enters forestry at gate and goes along the side of Dungoil then Dunbrach which has impressive cliffs. The road turns left, then right. There is a junction marked with forestry post C6 P73. Take right fork. There is a gully well below on the right as you go along. The road abruptly ends. You have to turn left through the trees and can do this either by going farther on for a short distance and turning up a narrow break, or going back and turning up a wider firebreak. At the end of either there is a fence signalling the end of the trees. Go over this and climb up to highest point which is the summit of Dunbrach. This is unmarked except for a few loose stones which was once perhaps a small cairn.

Now head SSE for Holehead. This is relatively flat ground, tufty and boggy in parts. Look for dyke and fence on skyline and make for where they apparently join. When you reach that point you will find a small gate in fence. Go through this, then along side of dyke until a little after it bends to the left. Cross it and go over to summit of Holehead (551m 1805f. TP. BM S3562).

Return to dyke, cross it, and go through small gate in fence. Then turn down alongside fence. Veer over to the left and make downhill (NE) to foot of Dungoil which from here looks very low. Well down, a fence is crossed. Near the bottom is forestry through which flows a burn with a fence running parallel on its near side. Follow this fence down until it turns across the burn, then follow the burn. When it levels out, cross it and go through break in trees and up to a forestry road. Turn right along it and then up through a firebreak to hillside and on to summit (over to left) of Dungoil (426m 1396f).

Leave the summit at the far (E) end, dropping steeply down on the right. Swing round to the left, going downhill steeply on grass to forestry. Turn along to left until firebreak. Go along this, which becomes steep downhill and narrow. At the end is a fence to be crossed. Then it is only a short distance down to the road where you started.

To shorten the walk, go from Dunbrach to Dungoil (omitting Holehead). Save 1.6km 1ml.

Ben Venue. Walk 24.

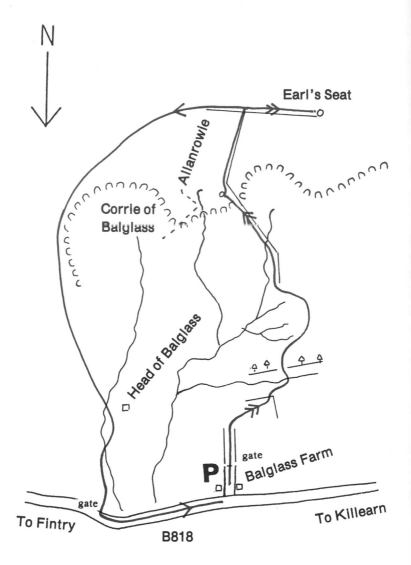

N

Earl's Seat

Allanrowie

Corrie of
Balglass

Head of Balglass

gate

Balglass Farm

P

To Fintry

gate

To Killearn

B818

WALK 10

10. Corrie of Balglass and Earl's Seat.

Ordnance Survey map 57. Distance from city centre to car parking: 33.6km 20.9ml. Walking distance from parking: 19km 11.8ml. Height of climbing: 548m 1797f. Can be quite a strenuous walk, but the views of the tremendous corries make it worth the effort.

Park car at Place of Balglass (Ballikinrain farm) on B818. NS580878. To get there, take A81 (via Canniesburn) to Blanefield, then A875 to Killearn, and B818 (Fintry road).

Walk S along old farm track for 0.8km 0.5ml. At its end turn towards the right and walk up to where two fences meet at right angles. Cross, then head for break in dyke (along which there are a few trees). Go through this break and again walk up towards the right and round the head of burns until a fence is reached. Turn up alongside this. It crosses a burn. Follow it, and it will lead you all the way to the top. Slightly to the left side is a cairn marking the height of 478m 1568f. It is worth diverging to go to this. Return to fence and follow it along side of small corrie, then a dip in the ground before rising on to Earl's Seat ridge. Here another fence is met at right angles. Turn right along this and walk up to Earl's Seat (578m 1896f. TP. BM S1622).

When returning, retrace your steps down by the fence, but do not turn left at junction. Continue down and up Allanrowie, although this is rough and wet land. Then circle E side of Corrie of Balglass. Note how clear the strata of the rock shows up. It is easy to imagine the time when the sea swirled round this enormous corrie. Fossils of sea creatures have been found here. In descending, head for point just E of Head of Balglass farm and follow track beside burn to road. Walk along road to car.

To shorten the walk, at top of path (near cairn) turn left and walk round corrie top and join return route (omitting Earl's Seat). Save 5.6km 3.5ml

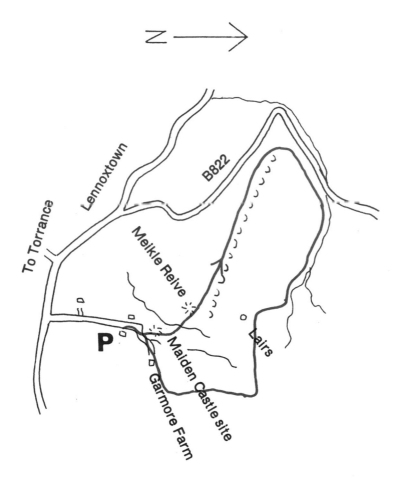

N →

Lennoxtown

B822

To Torrance

Meikle Reive

Maiden Castle site

Garmore Farm

Lairs

P

WALK 11

CAMPSIE FELLS— KILSYTH HILLS

11.   Meikle Reive and Lairs.

Ordnance Survey map 64. Distance from city centre to car parking: 16.4km 10.2ml. Walking distance from parking place: 13.2km 8.2ml. Height of climbing: 474m 1555f. Following the traces of an old road on the familiar Campsies. Note the scars of old limestone and coal workings. Full of interest.

Park car on road leading to Garmore farm. NS641773. To get there proceed via Bishopbriggs and Torrance to A891 (Milton of Campsie to Strathblane). Turn right (E) along A891 and turn first left.

Walk up road towards Garmore farm but, before reaching it, leave road on left and go towards a high piece of ground above a burn on its right. This is the site of Maiden Castle, which has been partly washed away over the centuries by the fast-flowing stream from the hill. Proceed NW to remains of Meikle Reive fort. The layout of this is quite clear. It is probably of Iron Age construction. From this point walk WNW keeping to the height of the fort as far as possible. When you come above the B822 road look out for track leading to remains of old road. This road will become clearer as you proceed. It runs parallel to but high above the B822, but below the cliffs. When it comes to the point above the large parking place at the turn of the road, the paths from below cross it. You should continue round the shoulder and follow the old road to near where it joins the B822 at a burn. Here turn E and follow the burn up its glen, then SSE to the top of Lairs (504m 1652f. Cairn).

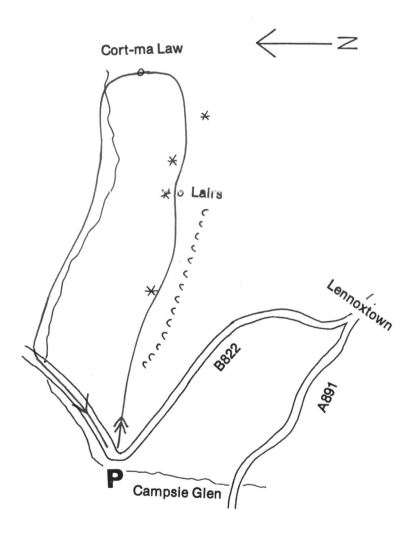

Cort-ma Law

Lairs

Lennoxtown

B822

A891

P Campsie Glen

WALK   12

From Lairs walk farther E and then descend near burn to Garmore farm and back to car.

To shorten the walk, return from point above parking place on B822, by outward route. Save 2.6km 1.6ml.

12.   Lairs and Cort-ma Law.

Ordnance Survey map 64. Distance from city centre to car parking: 19km 11.8ml. Walking distance from parking: 12.2km 7.6ml. Height of climbing: 332m 1089f. A typical Campsies plateau walk. Suitable for both summer and winter, but not in the rain.

Park car in car park on B822 (the Crow Road) above Campsie Glen. NS613801. To get there, go via Bishopbriggs, Torrance and Lennoxtown.

Cross road and climb steeply E along path which passes a cairn before coming to Lairs (504m 1652f. Cairn). Another cairn can be seen in the distance. Follow path along to this. Continue on path and a fourth cairn can be seen. The path, however, turns left and does not pass this cairn. Continue to Cort-ma Law (531m 1742f. TP. BM S3649). Return by going N over burn then W across moorland to where burn joins the Crow Road. Walk along road to car park.

To shorten the walk, return from Lairs by outward route. Save 5.6km 3.5ml.

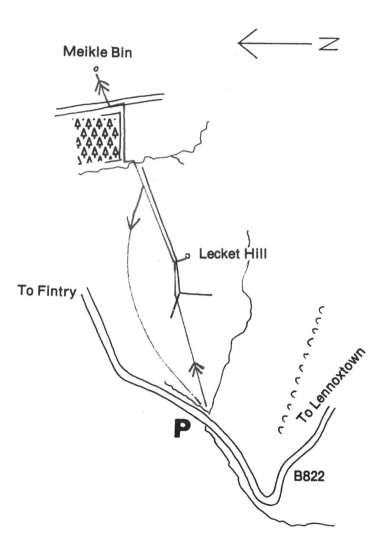

Meikle Bin

N

Lecket Hill

To Fintry

To Lennoxtown

P

B822

WALK   13

13. Lecket Hill and Meikle Bin.

Ordnance Survey map 64. Distance from city centre to car parking: 19.6km 12.2ml. Walking distance from parking: 14.2km 8.8ml. Height of climbing: 525m 1722f. A good walk for a sunny day to the highest point in the Kilsyth Hills.

Park car in lay-by on B822 (Lennoxtown to Fintry — the Crow Road) near bridge where road crosses burn. NS623807. To get there go via Bishopbriggs and Torrance.

Cross burn which flows beside road, before it joins burn from hills. (If this should prove difficult, walk back along road until past bridge. Then go back on hillside beside burn from hills until it can be crossed.) A path uphill is now evident. Follow this. At first it is steep, but it levels out and the summit of Lecket Hill can be seen. The path meets a fence coming up from the right and turning NE. Continue on path alongside fence until its highest point. (Note here, at turn of fence, an old boundary stone.) Cross the fence and walk short distance to summit of Lecket Hill (546m 1792f. Cairn).

Retrace your steps to path at fence and follow it steeply down to burn in gully. This is the Strathclyde/Central Regions boundary. Cross burn, turn left, walk along to start of older forest. Walk up side of this to forestry road. Turn left for a few steps, then right along path to summit of Meikle Bin (570m 1870f. TP. BM S3561).

Return by retracing your steps down to gully, but thereafter skirting to the N round Lecket Hill to avoid further climbing.

To shorten the walk, after passing Lecket Hill summit instead of going all the way down to burn skirt to left when half way down, and join return route. Save 6.4km 4ml.

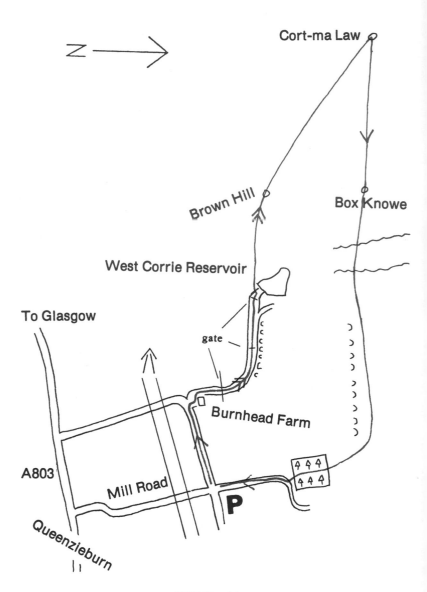

N →

Cort-ma Law

Brown Hill

Box Knowe

West Corrie Reservoir

To Glasgow

gate

Burnhead Farm

A803

Mill Road

P

Queenzieburn

WALK 14

14. Cort-ma Law and Box Knowe.

Ordnance Survey map 64. Distance from city centre to car parking: 18.7km 11.6ml. Walking distance from parking 13.2km 8.2ml. Height of climbing: 418m 1371f. This walk on the easterly part of the Kilsyth Hills is an interesting variation from others on the same hills. It is not at all difficult.

Park car at top of Mill Road going from Queenzieburn (which is on A803 about 2.5km 1.5ml W of Kilsyth). This is a T junction near Cairnbog. Park at corner or on hard shoulder to the E of T junction. NS690785. To get there go via Bishopbriggs and Kirkintilloch by-pass.

Walk WSW along road to Burnhead farm. Turn into farm. Walk in front of cottage then follow road to right uphill through a number of gates. The road will rise alongside a deep gully on the right. Near the top it divides. Take the left branch, then through a gate to dam. Climb to top of dam. You will now see what was West Corrie Reservoir but is now empty. Turn left along dam top then W over hills to Brown Hill (396m 1299f), and on NW to Cort-ma Law (531m 1742f. TP. BM S3649). Return E to Box Knowe (460m 1509f) a flat top. Still going E and crossing a number of burns make for shelf in hills just down from the top ridge (lower than this is very steep). At the end of this shelf, turn down into pleasant woodland. Go through this and out through gate to road, and so down to car.

To shorten the walk, go direct from Brown Hill to Box Knowe (omitting Cort-ma Law). Save 4.7km 2.9ml.

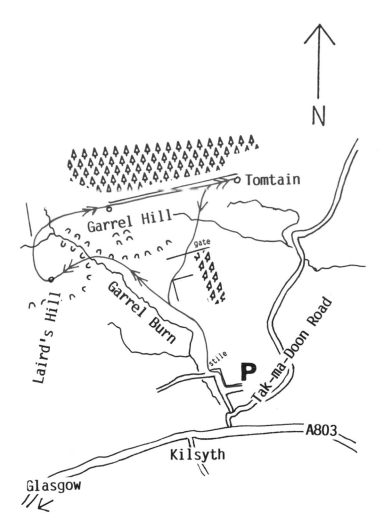

N

Tomtain

Garrel Hill

gate

Laird's Hill

Garrel Burn

Tak-ma-Doon Road

stile

P

A803

Kilsyth

Glasgow

WALK 15

15. Laird's Hill, Garrel Hill and Tomtain.

Ordnance Survey map 64. Distance from city centre to car parking: 21.1km 13.1ml. Walking distance from parking: 15.7km 9.8ml. Height of climbing: 466m 1528f. An easy walk on hills giving excellent views especially to the east over the widening River Forth and the Ochil Hills.

Park car in side road near entrance to Kilsyth and Lennox Golf Club. NS720787. To get there, go via Bishopbriggs, Kirkintilloch bypass and Kilsyth (A803). Just past the centre of Kilsyth turn left up Tak-ma-Doon Road. Immediately after it turns right, turn left up road to golf course.

Walk up the road which is continuation of road up which you motored. At top, turn left. Shortly after there is an entrance to field on right. Go through this and follow route of old path until just before narrow gorge. Cross Garrel Burn and climb up Laird's Hill (425m 1393f – not marked). Leave in N direction, descending and crossing Garrel Burn where a dyke comes down on other side. From here climb up and along to summit of Garrel Hill (458m 1503f – not marked). Then follow line of dyke along to summit of Tomtain (453m 1484f. TP. BM S3564).

Return by retracing steps to first bealach. There is an old stone here which was part of a demolished building, with the inscription 'Built in 1856 by A. Dennistoun'. Turn S and descend along route of old path (seldom discernible). Go through gate in wall coming from woodland, but avoiding next gate and going to right and down right side of fence. Join upward route.

To shorten this walk, omit the last ascent to Tomtain. Save 2.2km 1.4ml.

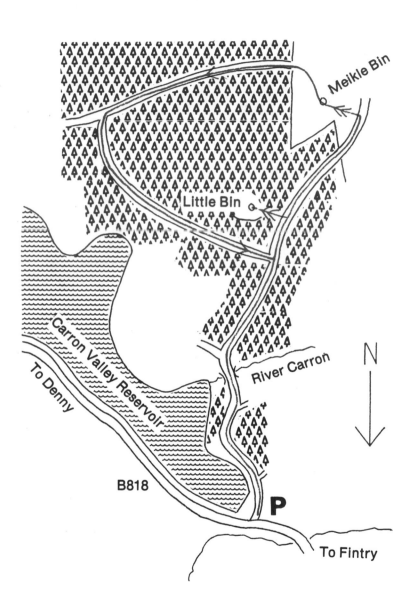

Meikle Bin

Little Bin

Carron Valley Reservoir

To Denny

River Carron

N

B818

P

To Fintry

WALK 16

16.   *Little Bin and Meikle Bin.*

Ordnance Survey map 57. Distance from city centre to car parking 31.7km 19.7ml. Walking distance from parking 18km 11.2ml. Height of climbing: 491m 1610f. Quite a long walk, but mostly on forest roads. Excellent views from top.

Park car at forestry road entrance on B818 (Fintry to Denny) at W end of Carron Valley Reservoir, and opposite Todholes. NS672858. This reservoir was built in 1939 and considerably raised the level of the small loch. To get there, go by Bishopbriggs, Torrance, Lennoxtown, then over the Crow Road, B822, turning right just before Fintry along B818 for 3.2km 2ml.

Walk along forestry road (ignoring two roads on the right) and cross bridge over River Carron. At first junction, go right. Further on there are two roads to the right. Take the second. When ascending road is about to level out and swing to left, look for firebreak on left, which will lead you to top of Little Bin (441m 1446f). Return down firebreak to forestry road and continue in the original direction along that road until rounding Meikle Bin. Leave road and strike up path for summit (570m 1870f. TP. BM S3561). Leave summit in SE direction, to find forestry road on left just over burn entering forest. Follow this road until first junction, when the left fork should be followed. This brings you back to outgoing road. Continue to car.

To shorten the walk, omit climb up Little Bin and return from Meikle Bin by outward route. Save 6.1km 3.8ml.

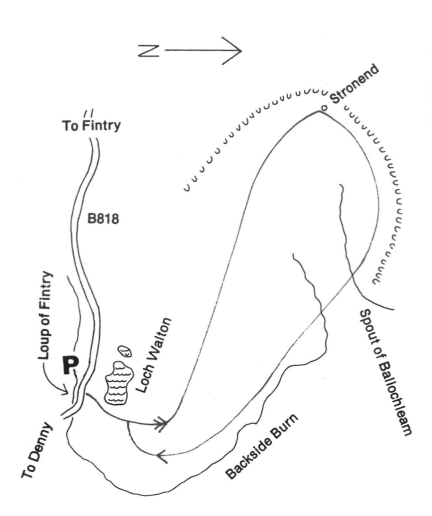

N →

To Fintry

B818

Loup of Fintry

To Denny

P

Loch Walton

Stronend

Spout of Ballochleam

Backside Burn

WALK 17

FINTRY, GARGUNNOCK AND TOUCH HILLS

17.   Stronend and Spout of Ballochleam.

Ordnance Survey map 57. Distance from city centre to car parking: 30.7km 19.1ml. Walking distance from parking: 20.3km 12.6ml. Height of climbing: 358m 1174f. A good high-level cover of the Fintry Hills.

Park car on B818 (Fintry to Denny) at or near entrance to Loch Walton. Leave the entrance free for angling club members' cars. NS664864. To get there, go by Bishopbriggs, Torrance, Lennoxtown, then over the Crow Road, B822, turning right just before Fintry along B818 for 3.1km 1.9ml.

Before going on this walk you may like to go through a gate in the dyke on the S side of the road, and walk over to the River Endrick. Here you will see the Loup of Fintry, one of the finest waterfalls of the area, especially after rain.

Walk down private road towards loch but veer right round loch and straight up hill. Near top, turn W and walk along ridge over small tops to Stronend (512m 1679f. TP. BM 10974). The pillar is disguised by pieces of natural stone fixed to its sides. Then proceed NE along edge and round to Spout of Ballochleam. Return along via SW side of Backside Burn, but turning S to meet route at start up hill. Return to car.

To shorten the walk, return from Stronend by outward route. Save 3km 1.9ml.

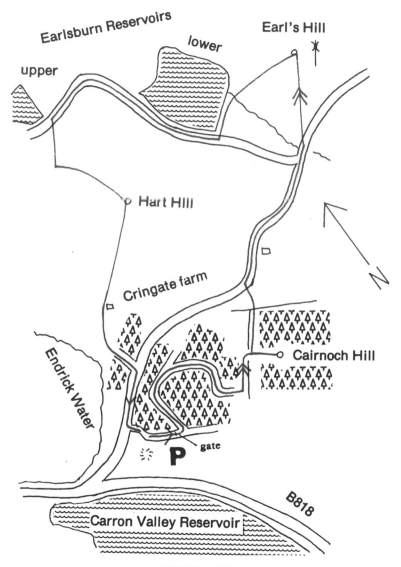

Earlsburn Reservoirs

upper

lower

Earl's Hill

Hart Hill

Cringate farm

Cairnoch Hill

Endrick Water

P

gate

N

B818

Carron Valley Reservoir

WALK 18

18.   *Cairnoch Hill, Earl's Hill and Hart Hill.*

Ordnance Survey map 57. Distance from city centre to car parking: 32.7km 20.3ml. Walking distance from parking: 20.3km 12.6ml. Height of climbing: 402m 1318f. A varied road, woodland, moorland walk — not too tiring.

Park car at Dundaff Castle remains near Carron Valley Reservoir. NS682858. (This 12th/13th century castle is also called 'Graham's Castle' after the owner Sir John the Graham, who was a friend of William Wallace. The latter often visited the castle. It was burned down by the English.) To get there see walk 17, but leave B818 1.5km 1ml farther E along road marked 'Except for access'. About 0.5km 0.3ml along this road turn right up rough forestry road. Park car about 90m 100y up this road at point overlooking castle grounds (grass with seats).

Start walk along forestry road going SE. At Y junction take left fork. Follow this road for quite a distance until there is a turn-off to the right. Go along this and it will eventually emerge from the forest and end at a dyke. Turn left along path at side of wall. Just past highest point, turn right through gap in wall opposite gap in forest. Proceed through gap and on to summit of Cairnoch Hill (413m 1355f. TP. BM 3647). Return to wall at start of gap through which you came. Follow the wall down to the right (N) until it reaches another wall at right angles at the foot of the small valley. Cross wall and fence (barbed and tricky) and go N to road. Proceed right along this road to bridge over river (at side road junction).

Climb NE to high masts which are at the summit of Earl's Hill (440m 1443f). These masts transmit a beam which is used by ships and aircraft for direction finding. The source of Bannock Burn is 0.8km 0.5ml N, but the ground here is heathery and marshy. Descend W to dam of lower Earlsburn Reservoir and cross this to road. Turn right along road to dam of upper Earlsburn Reservoir. Turn left off road and climb SW to top of

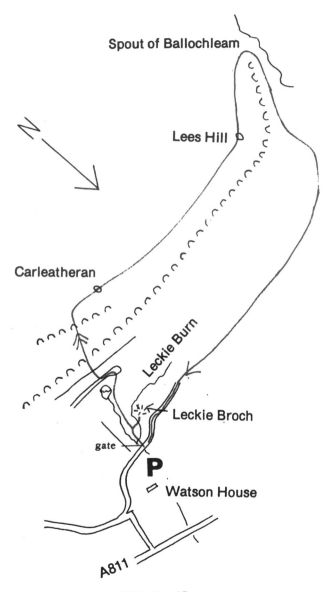

Spout of Ballochleam

Lees Hill

Carleatheran

Leckie Burn

Leckie Broch

gate

P

Watson House

A811

WALK 19

bealach then S to summit of Hart Hill (436m 1430f — not marked and not clear). Leave SW, descending well into valley and picking up tractor tracks, to ruined Cringate farm. (Just 0.8km 0.5ml NNW of here, the Endrick Water starts its journey to Loch Lomond.) From here the old road proceeds to and through forest to 'Except for access' road. Turn right, and shortly turn up left to forestry road and car.

To shorten the walk, on descending from Cairnoch Hill and reaching road, turn left along this to start. Save 11.3km 7ml.

19. Carleatheren and Lees Hill.

Ordnance Survey map 57. Distance from city centre to car parking: 53.9km 33.5ml. Walking distance from parking: 20.4km 12.7ml. Height of climbing: 439m 1440f. Quite a long walk, but full of interest, in the Gargunnock Hills.

Park car in side road from Gargunnock to Watson House, NS699947, or in private road from that point, at Leckie Burn. NS691942. To get there, motor to Gargunnock via M80 (Glasgow to Stirling) leaving at junction 9, along A872 towards Stirling, left at round-about, then left to Cambusbarron and on to A811 for 2km 1.25ml before turning left and going through Gargunnock.

Start walk from Leckie Burn by going through small gate on S side of road on to path at left (E) side of burn. After a short distance take path to right, crossing burn, and follow this up to large mound. This was a broch and is known generally as the 'Leckie Broch'. It is reckoned to be about 2000 years old. There are cup and ring markings on some of the rock. Retrace your steps back across burn to main path. Follow this up hill. Watch out for old reservoir on left (which is worth a slight diversion). The path joins a forestry road. Turn left along and up this for about 100m/100y. Strike through trees on right to old stone dyke. Go over this and make

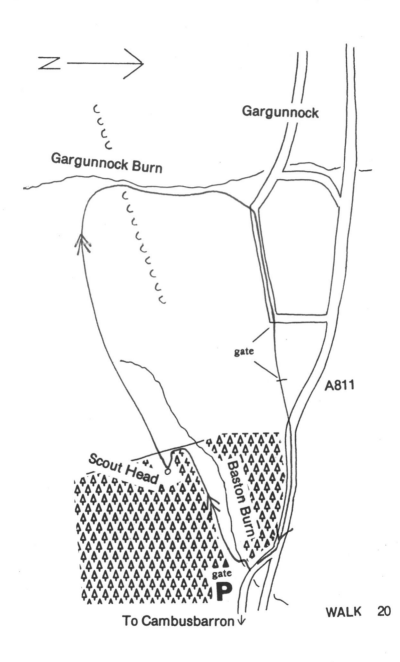

N →

Gargunnock

Gargunnock Burn

gate

A811

Scout Head

Baston Burn

gate

P

To Cambusbarron ↓

WALK   20

straight for hills. While the face is steep it is not difficult to find a way up and shortly you are on Carleatheren (485m 1591f. TP. BM S3633). Walk W along the edge for 2.5km 1.5ml to Lees Hill (411m 1348f). Return via Spout of Ballochleam, taking road down to just before Ballochleam farm, then striking NE overland to meet road at Leckie Burn.

To shorten the walk, return from Carleatheren by outward route. Save 14.5km 9ml.

20.   *Scout Head and Gargunnock Burn.*

Ordnance Survey map 57. Distance from city centre to car parking: 47.6km 29.6ml. Walking distance from parking: 15.6km 9.7ml. Height of climbing: 383m 1256f. A mixed woodland and hill top walk in the Touch (pronounced 'toosh') Hills. Not too long nor too high.

Park car at side of road (good space available) from Cambusbarron to Gargunnock 450m 500y before it joins A811. NS744938. To get there see walk 19, but stop earlier.

Go over gate and follow forest road short distance, then go through hedge and over burn into natural forest. Keep to left of Baston Burn and gradually climb upwards for some distance. Continue to wall at end of woodland. Do not cross wall. Turn left and follow wall until ground levels out, then strike back (left) into woodland and up to summit of Scout Head (215m 705f. TP. BM S3676). Return to wall, cross, and strike up ridge until you meet Gargunnock Burn. Follow burn down and at steep part locate and follow remains of old road (made originally to transport peat by sledge) down to Gargunnock. Walk E along road (partly on A811) to car.

To shorten the walk, return from head of Gargunnock Burn by outward route, but without going back to Scout Head. Save 3.7km 2.3ml.

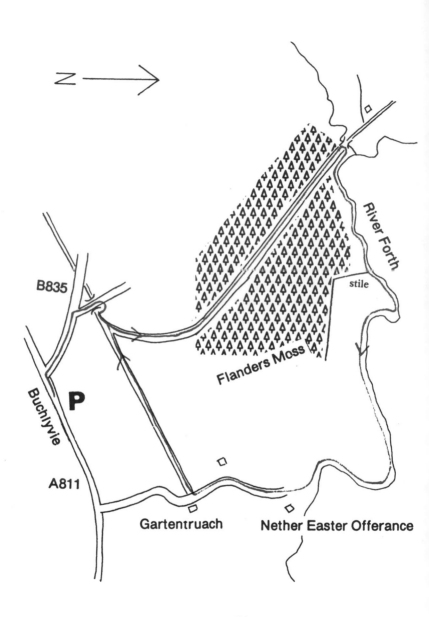

N →

B835

Buchlyvie

P

A811

Flanders Moss

River Forth

stile

Gartentruach

Nether Easter Offerance

WALK 21

21.   Flanders Moss.

Ordnance Survey map 57. Distance from city centre to car parking: 37.2km 23.1ml. Walking distance from parking: 19.1km 11.9ml. This is not a hill walk, but an outing for hill walkers when they feel like a level walk with time to sit beside a gently flowing river. It is interesting to note that Flanders Moss, stretching from the Firth of Forth to the mountains in the west, formed a barrier against invaders including the Romans. Before they came it was a rich alluvial plain, but about 210AD they destroyed a forest on it and it became a bog. Early in the 1800s the peat was skimmed off and floated down the River Forth to the sea, leaving land which could be cultivated.

The University of Glasgow hope to construct a gravitational-wave observatory in this area, with 36-inch-diameter pipes running for about a kilometre along the side of each of the rail tracks near where they join. The purpose is to monitor events in outer space.

Park car at lay-by near Buchlyvie. NS578939. To get there, take A81 (via Canniesburn) to Blanefield and continue through Killearn and Balfron to Buchlyvie. Just past the village and on the left side is an excellent lay-by, with toilets.

Walk back to the village, then turn right along B835. After 1km 0.6ml turn right along farm road. Go below old railway bridge, but climb up to rail track here. Follow track to the left (NE). It makes a long curve to the left (the Aberfoyle branch) then is straight between forest over Flanders Moss. After 2km 1.3ml of the straight road there is a bridge over a burn. Don't cross the bridge. Turn right off the road and follow the burn — there is a path but it can be overgrown. The burn flows into the River Forth after a very short distance and the path follows the river. There are very tall grasses here but there is no problem getting through. After about 1.8km 1.1ml, there is a stile over a fence. This starts a pleasant walk through meadows alongside the river. If the weather suits and you have the time, here is where you should sit and relax.

Continue alongside the river, past Over Easter Offerance — which is a ruin, to Nether Easter Offerance, then down the farm road to Gartentruach. Here turn right along the old railway line (the Stirling branch). Follow this, crossing a few fences, until it joins the Aberfoyle branch which you went along earlier. And so to the car.

To shorten the walk, keep on farm road after Gartentruach. Then along main road to car park. Save 3km 1.9ml.

Fintry Loup. Walk 17.

Looking across Loch Chon to Frenich and Beinn Uamha (top left). Walks 26 and 27.

On path round Loch Chon. Walk 26.

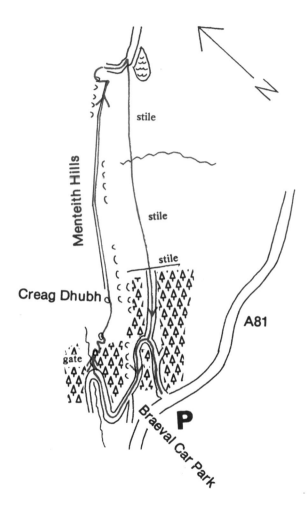

Menteith Hills

stile

stile

stile

Creag Dhubh

gate

A81

P

Braeval Car Park

WALK 22

ABERFOYLE AREA

22. Menteith Hills

Ordnance Survey map 57. Distance from city centre to car parking: 43.4km 27ml. Walking distance from parking: 15km 9.3ml. Height of climbing: 385m 1263f. Though not very high this walk gives very rewarding views. Steepish ups and downs, with some tufty heather. This is part of the geological line known as the Highland Boundary Fault. The name 'Menteith' means 'moorland of the Teith'.

Park car in Braeval forestry car park just off A81 (Glasgow to Callander via Canniesburn, Strathblane and Ballat) about 1.25km 0.75ml past Aberfoyle A821 road junction (Rob Roy Motel). NN543006.

Walk NE along forestry road following white way-marking, i.e. at first junction go left, at second also go left (i.e. not one marked 'To Callander'). This road bends to the left. At next junction go right, i.e. 'Lime Craigs'. The road will, later, turn right up a gully at the top of which it crosses and turns down the other side. Before that turn, look for path (it looks like a small burn) on right. Go up this — it soon becomes a recognisable path — on right side of main burn. Pass through a gate. Follow path, keeping up to the right by zig-zags to top of first hill. The TP on top of Creag Dhubh can then be seen. Find track on your right which goes down into gully then up and round S side to summit

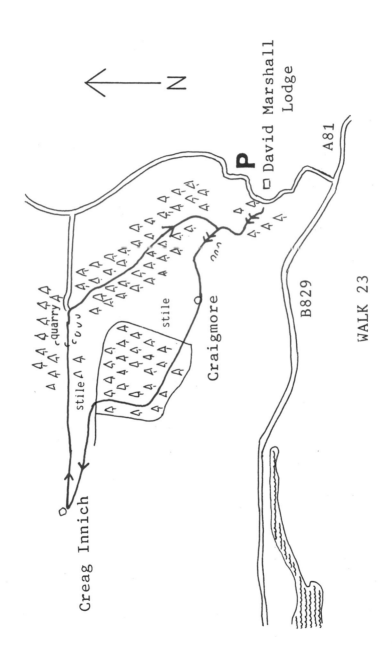

N

Creag Innich

quarry

stile

stile

Craigmore

David Marshall
Lodge

P

A81

B829

WALK 23

of Creag Dhubh (400m 1312f. TP. BM S6760). On a clear day especially the views are magnificent.

From here the walk continues along the ridge in an easterly direction, following a fence. It is mainly tufty heather and there are a few steep descents and ascents especially at the start.

Near the end of the long ridge descend to the left (N) and round through a gap, to front and bottom of the ridge. Keep going E to forestry road. Turn right along this for a short distance and, when you see a small loch on your right, look for right-of-way path going back on the right. Turn along this path and follow it all the way (5km 3ml) back to car park.

To shorten the walk, go down from a low part about half way along a ridge to the return journey path. Save 3.7km 2.3ml.

23. Craigmore and Creag Innich.

Ordnance Survey map 57. Distance from city centre to car parking: 45km 28ml. Walking distance from parking: 10.5km 6.5ml. Height of climbing: 400m 1312f. A mixture of walking over high-level plateau and along old track among trees.

Park car at David Marshall Lodge (gifted to the Forestry Commission in 1960). NN518015. To get there see walk 24 for route to Rob Roy Motel. Turn left along A821 to Aberfoyle, then turn right there (i.e. continue on A821) and zig-zag up hill to lodge entrance on right.

Walk back to road, turn right and at first bend find a path leaving the other side and going steeply uphill. This path can be difficult to find when overgrown in summer and autumn. It is also advisable to wear waterproof leggings and jacket at that season. Climb this route, crossing a stiled fence on the way, to end of abandoned rail track from quarries. Continue upwards and on to Craigmore (387m 1269f). From here walk NW to Creag Innich (522m 1712f). This is rough heathery ground, and deer fences have been erected. There are some high

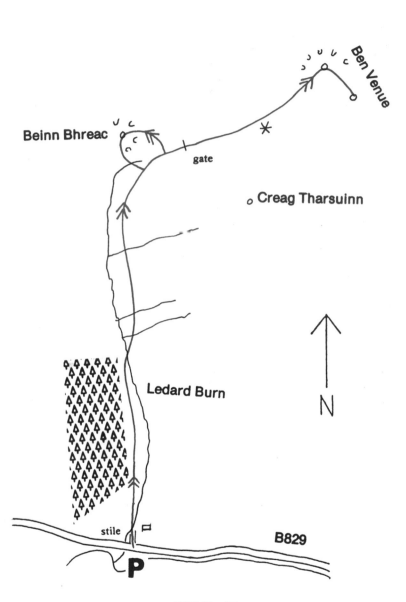

Ben Venue

Beinn Bhreac

gate

Creag Tharsuinn

N

Ledard Burn

stile

B829

P

WALK 24

stiles but these might be avoided by going round the fence to the right. Do not attempt to descend by forestry road going towards Loch Ard since it will take you out at Forest Hills which is many miles from your car. Return ESE finding a burn which you can follow through the woods on to a stone pile being part of the Aberfoyle Quarries (at one time there was a greater population living at these quarries than in Aberfoyle village). Once onto the quarry road, follow this down to the last bend. At this point look for the remains of a level track off to the right, going over a stream and into the woods. Go along this. You will soon find that this old rail track is cut into in three places by quarrying, but on each occasion there is a path up and round the intrusion. After these it is simply a case of following the track back to its end which you passed early in your walk, and so down to car.

To shorten the walk, go from Craigmore across to quarry (omitting Creag Innich). Save 3km 1.9ml.

24. Ben Venue and Beinn Bhreac.

Ordnance Survey map 57. Distance from city centre to car parking: 51km 31.7ml. Walking distance from parking: 18.3km 11.4ml. Height of climbing: 815m 2673f. A popular walk, fully justified because of the scenery and the view from the top. Despite the distance the upward path makes it less strenuous.

Park car in lay-by on B829 (Aberfoyle to Inversnaid) at Ledard, just before end of Loch Ard. NN461023. To get there take A81 (Glasgow to Callander via Canniesburn, Strathblane and Ballat), but turn left at Rob Roy Motel along A821 to Aberfoyle. In Aberfoyle go straight through onto B829 (rather than continuing on A821 which turns right, up hill). Continue for 6.2km 3.9ml.

Walk up farm road opposite lay-by, over stile and small bridge, and up path (waymarked with green chevrons). This passes Ledard waterfall and pool on your right. When above tree level and after the path crosses the Ledard Burn, watch that you take the higher

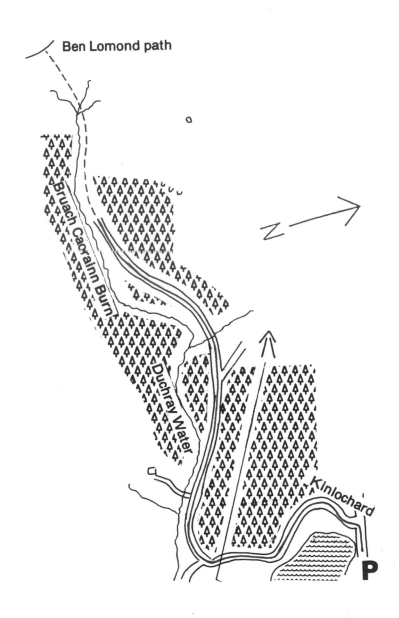

Ben Lomond path

Bruach Caoralnn Burn

Duchray Water

Kinlochard

P

WALK 25

path, which will lead you between Beinn Bhreac and Creag Tharsuinn. Then at a waymark cairn, the route is joined by the path from Loch Achray. Continue up to the twin tops of Ben Venue (727m 2386f. TP. BM S6961m and 729m 2393f) — 'the hill of young cattle'. Return to bealach between Creag Tharsuinn and Beinn Bhreac. Turn right and ascend to summit of Beinn Bhreac — 'the speckled ben'. Forestry prevents a descent down the ridge from this hill, so you will have to return to bealach and go down the path to start.

To shorten the walk, omit Beinn Bhreac. Save 2.1km 1.3ml.

25.   Kinlochard towards Rowardennan.

Ordnance Survey maps 57 and 56. Distance from city centre to car parking: 51km 31.7ml. Walking distance from parking: 22.5km 14ml. Height of climbing: 250m 820f. This is a walk for those days when the weather puts you off going to the open tops of the hills.

Park car at Ledard. NN461023. See walk 24.

Walk W to Kinlochard (about 400m 440y) then turn left. Follow signs for 'Rowardennan' (waymarked with red chevrons). This pleasant forestry road winds through tree-covered country surrounded by hills, for a long way. Keep watching for the signs as there are a number of branches. After 11.3km 7ml the road ends. Here is a beautiful cascading burn. Turn here and go back by the same route.

The walk could be extended along a track (can be very muddy) which continues alongside of burn. It latterly emerges from the woodlands and contours the early shoulder of the Ben Lomond ridge. It joins the route up the Ben. To do this, however, would add 9km 5.5ml to your outing.

This walk can be shortened by turning back whenever you wish.

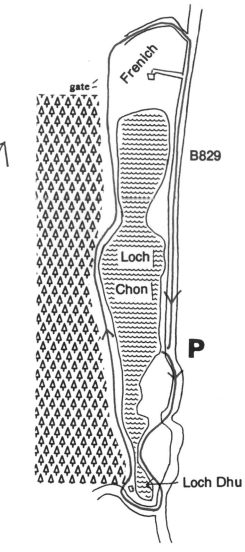

gate

Frenich

B829

Loch
Chon

P

 Loch Dhu

WALK 26

26.   *Round Loch Chon.*

Ordnance Survey map 56. Distance from city centre to car parking: 54.2km 33.7ml. Walking distance from parking: 12.2km 7.6ml. Height of climbing: 40m 131f. A pleasant level walk for a day when the hills are not an attraction. This has been forestry country since 1794. The name means 'the lake of the dogs'.

Park car at Loch Chon car park. NN426046. To get there see walk 24, but continue farther until sign for car park.

Walk back along road to sign for boathouse. Go down to loch side and turn left along shore before rejoining road at Loch Dhu. After 360m 400y turn right along Loch Dhu House road. After passing that house follow path up through trees marked 'Inversnaid via south side of Loch Chon'. This will take you down to side of loch. Watch for waymarked white chevrons. The path continues all the way, through forest, along the W side of the loch, with evidence (bridges, aqueducts) that it is a pipe track alongside pipes carrying water from Loch Katrine to Glasgow. Near the end of the loch the path leads through two small gates, then continues to the NW of Frenich and to public road B829. Turn right along road but leaving it when possible to walk along loch side. Arrive at car park.

It is not practicable to shorten this walk.

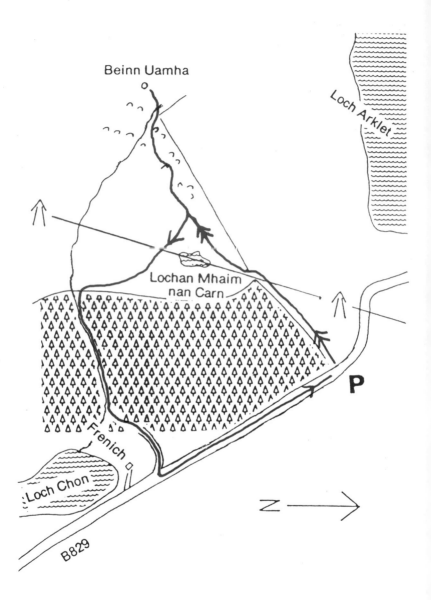

Beinn Uamha

Loch Arklet

Lochan Mhaim
nan Carn

P

Frenich

Loch Chon

Z ⟶

B829

WALK 27

27. *Beinn Uamha.*

Ordnance Survey map 56. Distance from city centre to car parking: 58.6km 36.4ml. Walking distance from parking: 12.4km 7.7ml. Height of climbing: 528m 1732f. A moderate climb on rough, heathery, ground among many rocky knobs; and ending with a walk through a forestry firebreak then a road. Do not attempt in mist or snow. 'Uamha' means 'cave' or 'hollow'.

Park car on B829 (Aberfoyle to Inversnaid) at cattle grid at end of woodland 2.5km 1.5ml past Loch Chon. NN405087. To get there see walk 24, but continue farther.

Leave on SW side of road, crossing low fence, and after short fall, strike up hill alongside a high fence. When that fence turns left and a low fence carries on, cross the low fence (near the overhead electricity lines). Follow the line of the pylons but keep to the right of them. You will soon see the Lochan Mhaim nan Carn. Turn towards the right. You will see the low fence which is going towards the top, but as it follows a very steep up and down route keep sufficiently away from it to avoid difficulties. However, keep gaining height while going round various large knobs, and keep the fence in sight.

Before the top, the fence turns away to the right. Leave it at this point and go to the last of the various tops which is the summit of Beinn Uamha (598m 1962f. Small cairn). As you approach, you get a wonderful view of the N face of Ben Lomond, not to mention the panorama all round.

Check carefully the direction when leaving the top. Head for Loch Katrine and look for the fence which you left. Retrace your route (farther right are steep faces) until near lochan, then turn right and across below electricity lines to fence round forestry. Turn right along fence. Opposite the third pylon from the Lochan and at a burn, there is an opening in the fence and a firebreak through the trees. A burn flows into this break. Follow the burn keeping to its left side along traces of a path. After about 1.5km 1ml the path turns to the left and almost immediately joins the route round Loch Chon near one of the two small gates.

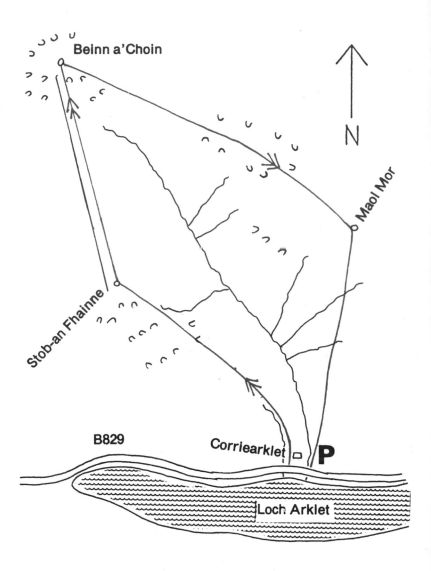

Beinn a'Choin

Maol Mor

Stob-an Fhainne

N

B829

Corriearklet

P

Loch Arklet

WALK   28

Go left and continue along path and road until the main road. Turn left and walk 1.5km 1ml to car.

To shorten walk, return from summit by outward route. Save 4.1km 2.5ml.

28.   *Beinn a' Choin.*

Ordnance Survey map 56. Distance from city centre to car parking: 63.7km 39.6ml. Walking distance from parking: 14.2km 8.8ml. Height of climbing: 811m 2660f. Quite a strenuous walk, but straightforward and well worth the effort.

Park car on road near Corriearklet at Loch Arklet on B829 (Aberfoyle to Inversnaid). NN375095. (There was once a village here.) To get there see walk 24, but continue for farther 8km 5ml to Loch Arklet, then turn left.

Strike up hill to left until summit of Stob-an Fhainne (652m 2139f). Continue along ridge, following fence across bealach, to Beinn a' Choin (769m 2522f) which is a Corbett. Return by SE to summit of Maol Mor (684m 2244f. TP. BM S6933), then down to car.

To shorten the walk, turn right at bealach to join return route (omitting Beinn a' Choin). Save 3.1km 1.9ml.

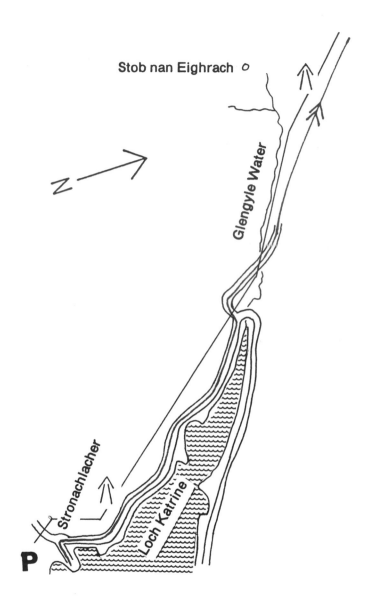

Stob nan Eighrach o

Glengyle Water

Stronachlacher

Loch Katrine

P

WALK 29

29.   Glen Gyle.

Ordnance Survey map 56. Distance from city centre to car parking: 62.6km 38.9ml. Walking distance from parking: 27km 16.8ml. Height of climbing: 290m 951f. A level walk along Loch Katrine waterworks road then old road up the glen. A longish car journey with an easy walk among magnificent hills in a perfect setting.

Park car at Stronachlacher pier on Loch Katrine. NN405103. To get there see walk 24, but continue for farther 8km 5ml to Loch Arklet then turn right. At foot of small slope, turn right along to pier.

Walk back from pier to entry to private road then right along that road going N to side of the loch. Loch Katrine is the main source of Glasgow's water supply. Follow this road to the end of the loch (about 4km 2.5ml). Turn left along old road which rises onto hill a little before going up the glen and over Glengyle Water. The glen is where Rob Roy MacGregor, second son of the chieftain, Colonel Donald MacGregor of Glengyle, was born. Follow the glen up to where the burn ends, then up to its head. Return by same route to car.

To shorten the walk, return after 1.6km 1ml up Glen Gyle. Save 9.8km 6.1ml.

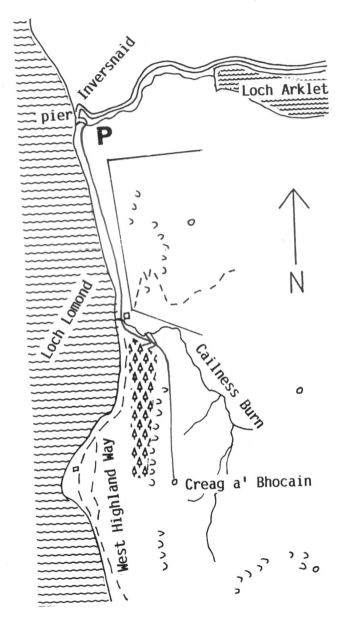

Inversnaid

pier

P

Loch Arklet

N

Loch Lomond

Cailness Burn

West Highland Way

Creag a' Bhocain

WALK 30

30.   Creag a' Bhocain.

Ordnance Survey map 56. Distance from city centre to car parking: 68km 42ml. Walking distance from parking: 16.2km 9.9ml. Height of climbing: 482m 1581f. A walk along the West Highland Way, then a short, sharp climb to get excellent view over Loch Lomond.

Park car at Inversnaid pier. NN337089. To get to Inversnaid see walk 24, but continue to Loch Arklet, then turn left for about 5.6km 3.4ml.

Walk along the West Highland Way path S for about 2.8km 1.7ml until Cailness Burn. Cross this and climb steeply to end of ridge. Follow S along ridge to summit of Creag a' Bhocain (492m 1614f). Return by same route.

It is not practicable to shorten this walk.

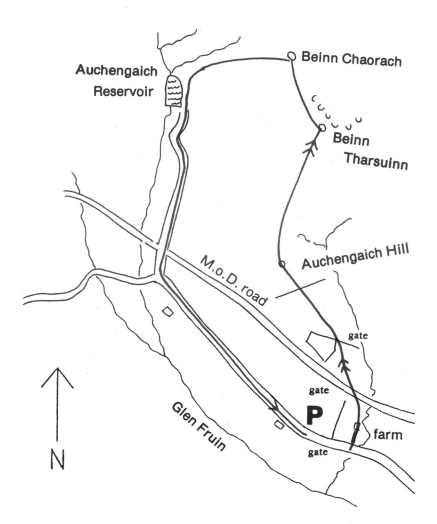

Auchengaich Reservoir

Beinn Chaorach

Beinn Tharsuinn

Auchengaich Hill

M.o.D. road

Glen Fruin

gate

gate

gate

P

farm

N

WALK   31

LOCH LOMOND WEST GLENS

31. Beinn Tharsuinn and Beinn Chaorach from Glen Fruin.

Ordnance Survey map 56. Distance from city centre to car parking: 42.8km 26.6ml. Walking distance from parking: 14.8km 9ml. Height of climbing: 626m 2053f. A good climb on firm ground. Delightful exercise. Don't let the desecration of this valley by temporary M.o.D. road put you off. Once above the first top it will be out of sight.

Park car in Glen Fruin road, just past Ballevoulin farm. NS293885. To get there, go by A82 (Loch Lomond W side road) to about 4km 2.5ml past Balloch roundabout, then turn left along B831, cross B832 and proceed on minor road up Glen Fruin.

Go through farm gate, up side of dyke, cross fences of M.o.D. road (look for gates), then up side of forestry. After going through gate in fence at top of forestry turn left along ridge. There is another fence to cross, and a few false tops, before reaching Auchengaich Hill (formerly Auchinvennel Hill) (512m 1680f). This is not marked and is the end of a broad grassy ridge. Continue on an almost level N direction along path (indistinct at times) before going through peat outcrop and ascending Beinn Tharsuinn (655m 2149f. Cairn). Go NNW down and up (indistinct path), avoiding cliffs on right, passing a small cairn, to summit of Beinn Chaorach (713m 2339f.

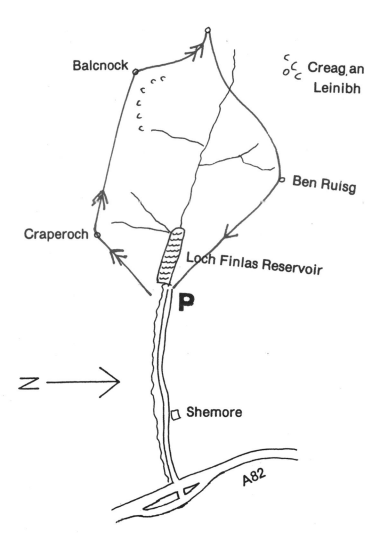

Balcnock

Creag an
Leinibh

Ben Ruisg

Craperoch

Loch Finlas Reservoir

P

N →

Shemore

A82

WALK   32

TP. BM S5080. Cairn). Return by dropping down to Auchengaich Reservoir, then by reservoir road, crossing M.o.D. road, to glen road and back to car. There is a monument to a clan battle which was fought where the Auchengaich Burn meets the Fruin Water. This was between the Colquhouns and the MacGregors in 1603.

To shorten the walk, after summit of Beinn Tharsuinn, return by outward route. Save 4.6km 2.8ml.

32.   The Loch Finlas Trio.

Ordnance Survey map 56. Distance from city centre to car parking: 38.9km 24.2ml. Walking distance from parking: 13.2km 8.2ml. Height of climbing: 617m 2024f. After the initial ascent, it is a wonderful high-level walk with magnificent views.

Park car at Loch Finlas reservoir. NS330894. To get there, leave A82 (Loch Lomond W side road) 1.2km 0.75ml N of junction with B832, along road signposted 'Shemore', i.e. along new M.o.D. road for 40m then turn right along old Shemore road. Motor to end of road – 2.5km 1.5ml – poor surface at start.

Climb steadily WSW to Craperoch, then NW to Balcnock (638m 2092f). Follow watershed round to unnamed top (693m 2273f), the highest point of the walk, then on to Creag an Leinibh (658m 2158f). Return by Beinn Ruisg (593m 1946f), then descending at an angle from the ridge to the car.

To shorten the walk, return by outward route from Balcnock. Save 3.5km 2.2ml.

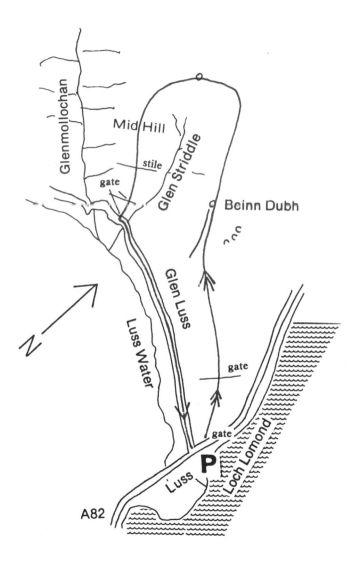

Glenmollochan

Mid Hill

Glen Striddle

stile

gate

Beinn Dubh

Glen Luss

Luss Water

N

gate

Loch Lomond

gate

P

gate

Luss

A82

WALK   33

33. Beinn Dubh and the horseshoe.

Ordnance Survey map 56. Distance from city centre to car parking: 41.4km 25.7ml. Walking distance from parking: 15km 9.3ml. Height of climbing: 692m 2270f. A steady, but not difficult, climb from an easy parking place, then a top-level walk with excellent views all around. Mostly walking on firm flat ground with lots of small paths. This is the television series 'Take the High Road' country.

Park car in car park at Luss. NS359931. To get there, go by A82 (Loch Lomond W side road) to Luss village.

Cross the main road and go over gate to the right of Glen Luss road. From here veer over to the right, climbing all the time. Look for path. Go over a gate in a fence. Keep to the centre of ridge. Paths will be found from time to time. There are a few false tops, and you join a fence which leads up to the summit of Beinn Dubh (643m 2109f).

Unless there is mist, you should now see the horseshoe, curving to the left around Glen Striddle, round which you will walk. Continue NW along ridge and round to unnamed top (655m 2148f), then to Mid Hill. The descent down ridge is pleasant. Cross a fence by a stile, and near the foot a gate in a dyke, then another gate into the road near Glenmollochan. Walk down Glen Luss road, a beautiful glen, to the village and your car.

To shorten the walk, return from Beinn Dubh by outward route. Save 4.8km 3ml.

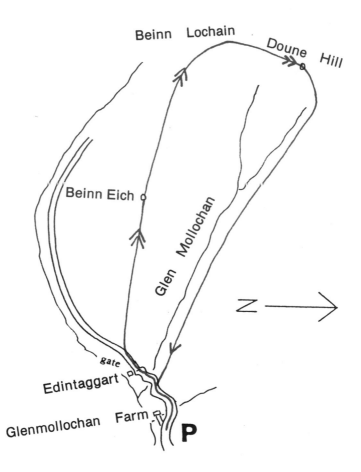

Beinn Lochain

Doune Hill

Beinn Eich

Glen Mollochan

N

gate

Edintaggart

Glenmollochan Farm

P

WALK 34

34. Beinn Eich and Doune Hill from Glen Luss.

Ordnance Survey map 56. Distance from city centre to car parking: 44.2km 27.5ml. Walking distance from parking: 16.1km 10ml. Height of climbing: 757m 2483f. A stiff pull-up, but well worth it. Hills all around.

Park car near Glenmollochan Farm 3.25km 2ml up Glen Luss road. NS329943. To get there, go by A82 (Loch Lomond W side road) to Luss. Turn left up Glen Luss road.

Walk along road to Edintaggart crossing two bridges over 200 years old. Strike on to Beinn Eich and climb steadily to summit (702m 2302f). Follow along ridge of Beinn Lochain onto Doune Hill (734m 2408f. TP. BM S8848). Walk NE a short distance to take in the second top of Doune Hill (699m 2298f). Return by descending to head of Glen Mollochan and along glen to car.

To shorten the walk, return from Beinn Eich by outward route, omitting Doune Hill. Save 7.2km 4.5ml.

Beinn Eich. Walk 34.

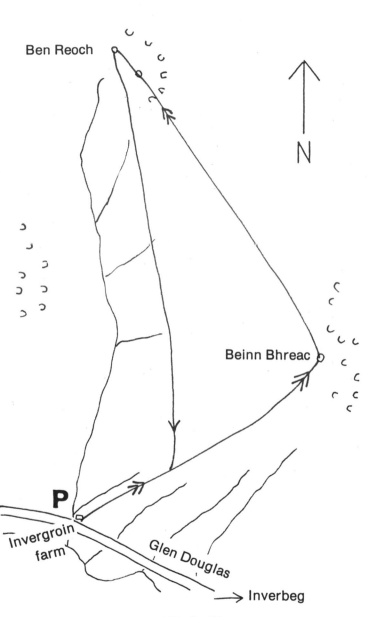

Ben Reoch

Beinn Bhreac

N

P

Invergroin
farm

Glen Douglas

 Inverbeg

WALK 35

35. Beinn Bhreac and Ben Reoch.

Ordnance Survey map 56. Distance from city centre to car parking: 50km 31.1ml. Walking distance from parking: 11.7km 7.3ml. Height of climbing: 801m 2627f. Quite a climb into country seldom reached by walkers.

Park car near Invergroin Farm in Glen Douglas. NS307989. To get there, go by A82 (Loch Lomond W side road) to Inverbeg. Turn left up Glen Douglas road.

Climb steadily to summit of Beinn Bhreac (681m 2233f) — 'the speckled ben', then along ridge to twin peaks of Ben Reoch (632m 2073f, and 661m 2186f). Return by descending gradually to meet outward route about half way up Beinn Bhreac and so to car.

To shorten the walk, return from Beinn Bhreac by outward route. Save 6.6km 4.1ml

Summit of Ben Uamha. Walk 27.

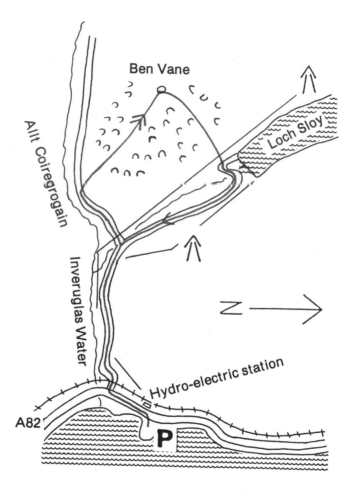

Ben Vane

Loch Sloy

Allt Coiregrogain

Inveruglas Water

N

Hydro-electric station

A82

P

WALK 36

36.   Ben Vane (Loch Sloy).

Ordnance Survey map 56. Distance from city centre to car parking: 60.5km 37.6ml. Walking distance from parking: 17.5km 10.9ml. Height of climbing: 900m 2952f. It used to be possible to take a car up to the dam, but now there is a long road to walk to add to the climb. This means a rather hard day, but for the strong it is worth it. Its name either means 'the white peak', or 'mountain of the river'. It is a Munro.

Park car at picnic site on loch side of A82 (Loch Lomond W side road) just past Inveruglas hydro-electric station. NN322099. To get there take A82 (Loch Lomond road) to about 5km 3.2ml past Tarbet.

Walk back along road to entrance to Loch Sloy private road. Walk along this private road for about 2km 1.2ml, until there is a branch on left over a river (Inveruglas Water). Take this branch and at its height (about 600m 700y) strike to the right up hill to summit of Ben Vane (916m 3004f). This is a very steep climb. Return N and E to dam at Loch Sloy, then along road back to the start.

To shorten the walk, return from Ben Vane by outward route. Save 1.9km 1.1ml.

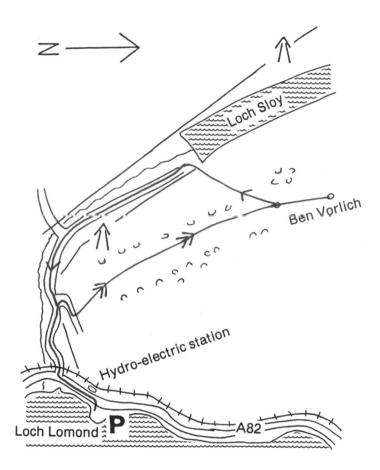

WALK 37

37. Ben Vorlich (Loch Sloy).

Ordnance Survey map 56. Distance from city centre to car parking: 60.5km 37.6ml. Walking distance from parking: 17.1km 10.6ml. Height of climbing: 928m 3044f. A long steady climb to a most interesting double top, returning on dam road. The name of the mountain means 'peak of the sea-bag'. It is a Munro.

Park car near Inveruglas hydro-electric station. NN322099. See walk 36.

Walk back along A82 road to entrance to Loch Sloy private road. Walk along private road for about 700m 750y then strike NW (to the right) up hill to ridge. Go along ridge to summit of Ben Vorlich (943m 3092f. TP. 100m 110y S. BM S6510), then a short distance N along summit ridge to second top (931m 3054f). Go back to summit and return S to dam of Loch Sloy, then by private road and A82 to start.

It is not practicable to shorten this walk, unless you are extremely lucky enough to get a hitch on a car or van along the private road.

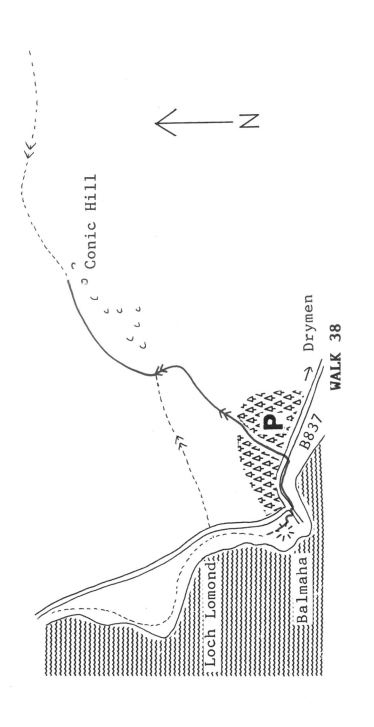

LOCH LOMOND — EAST SIDE

38.   Conic Hill.

Ordnance Survey map 56. Distance from city centre to car parking: 34.3km 21.2ml. Walking distance from parking: 5km 3ml. Height of climbing: 400m 1310f. An easy, short, but interesting walk, on the Highland Boundary Fault. Avoid this route during the lambing season, as part of it will be closed at that time.

Park car in Balmaha car park. NS421909. To get there, go by A809 (Bearsden to Drymen). At Drymen turn left along B837 to Balmaha. The large car park is on the right near the start of the village.

This walk is along the route of the West Highland Way. Leave the car park at the rear exit. Turn right along the path and climb the long line of steps. The height of Conic Hill is 358m 1174f.

You now have alternatives. You can continue eastwards along the Way and return, but this has little scenic attraction. It would be better to return to the car park and follow the Way route through the village, walking on the board path between the road and the Loch. The route then is up a steep path to the top of the hill above the pier on one side and the Pass of Balmaha on the other. Here you have an excellent view over Loch

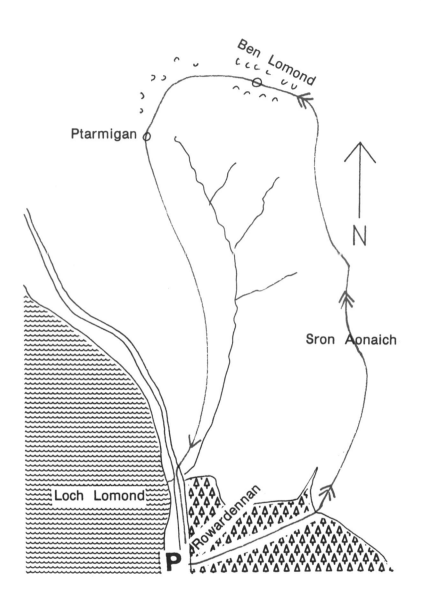

Ben Lomond

Ptarmigan

N

Sron Aonaich

Loch Lomond

Rowardennan

P

WALK 39

Lomond. Again you can continue north along the Way, or return to the car park.

On the Ordnance Survey map there is marked a path from near the top on Conic Hill going down the ridge in a south westerly direction and joining the Walk near the loch. However, the landowners state that to use it their permission is required.

To shorten this walk, after summit take Way path down to car park. Save 0.3km 0.2ml and a climb up to Craigie Fort.

39.   Ben Lomond.

Ordnance Survey map 56. Distance from city centre to car parking: 45.1km 28ml. Walking distance from parking: 16.6km 10.3ml. Height of climbing: 950m 3116f. This is a popular outing and so you will be walking on a too well-worn path, but it is really a fine hill walk. The top is magnificent and the descent via Ptarmigan a good finale. The name means 'beacon hill'. It is the most southerly Munro, and is now owned by the National Trust for Scotland.

Park car at Rowardennan car park. NS360987. To get there see walk 38, but continue past Balmaha.

Walk directly from the car park by path clearly signposted and marked. The route goes through forest then open land via Sron Aonaich (577m 1893f) to summit of Ben Lomond (974m 3192f. TP. BM S1594). The last part is narrow, so be careful.

Return by dropping down steep path at summit NW and round to summit of Ptarmigan (731m 2398f). Thence by easy descent along path (not always visible) along ridge until it drops down to meet rough road near loch side, about 1km 0.6ml from car park.

It is not practicable to shorten this walk, other than by turning back before reaching Ben Lomond summit.

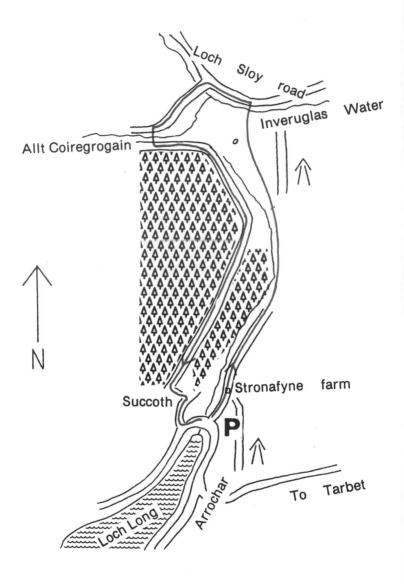

WALK 40

ARROCHAR AREA

40. Glen Loin.

Ordnance Survey map 56. Distance from city centre to car parking: 57.9km 36ml. Walking distance from parking: 16.6km 10.3ml. Height of climbing: 301m 987f. A low-level walk among the hills mostly on road or path. Keep it for a wet day.

Park car at start of road up Glen Loin at head of Loch Long on A83. NN298052. To get there take A82 (Loch Lomond W side road) to Tarbet, then fork left to Arrochar.

Walk N along farm road, through Stronafyne Farm, and continue until road becomes a track. Skirt E side of Dubh Chnoc. Drop down to Inveruglas Water, and cross it on to Loch Sloy road. (If the burns are in spate, do not cross Inveruglas Water. Keep round to left until the point where you would have crossed the Allt Coiregrogain.) Go NW along this road for a short distance until a branch on left goes over the river. Take this branch and follow for 1km 0.6ml. Leave road on left, drop down and over Allt Coiregrogain, then up through trees to forestry road. Turn left along this road which will lead you to Succoth, then a short distance to car.

To shorten the walk, return from Dubh Chnoc by outward route. Save 6.1km 3.8ml.

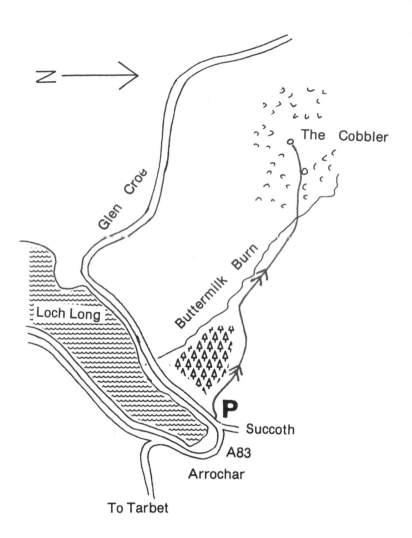

N →

The Cobbler

Glen Croe

Buttermilk Burn

Loch Long

P

Succoth

A83

Arrochar

To Tarbet

WALK 41

41.   Ben Arthur (The Cobbler).

Ordnance Survey map 56. Distance from city centre to car parking: 58.2km 36.2ml. Walking distance from parking: 11.3km 7ml. Height of climbing: 872m 2860f. A stiff, longish ascent to the spectacular summit which is a favourite of rock-climbers, but hill walkers can enjoy it just as much. It is a Corbett.

Park car at Succoth road end parking place on A83 at far (W) side of the head of Loch Long. NN293049. To get there, see walk 40, but continue a short distance farther.

Find path going S from parking place. Follow this. It quickly turns uphill and goes round top of woodland to meet path alongside Allt a' Bhalachain ('Buttermilk Burn'). Keep climbing up this path to summit. The Cobbler has three tops, the centre of which is the highest (881m 2891f). To get on to summit ridge, go up steep grass and scree slopes on either side of the centre peak. Once on the ridge the slope is gentle, but it is climaxed by a short tunnel on to a ledge and up from that to top. This requires considerable care and should only be undertaken by those with a good head for heights.

The north top is called 'The Cobbler's Wife' and is very impressive. It is easy to climb. The south top, 'The Cobbler's Last', is not suitable for other than experienced rock climbers. Return by same route.

It is not practicable to shorten this walk, except by turning back before reaching target.

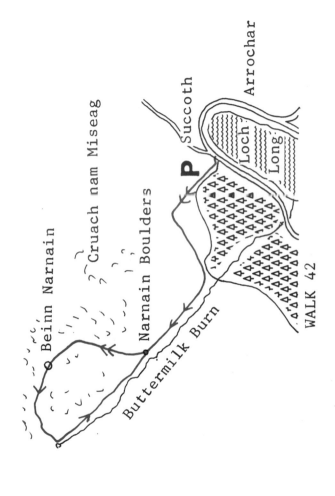

42. Beinn Narnain.

Ordnance Survey map 56. Distance from city centre to car parking: 58.2km 36.2ml. Walking distance from parking: 15km 9.3ml. Height of climbing: 916m 3004ft. A steep climb to the highest of the 'Arrochar Alps', which is a Munro.

Park car at Succoth road end parking place. NN293049. See Walk 41.

Find path going from parking place. Follow this. It quickly turns uphill and goes round top of woodland to meet path alongside Allt a' Bhalachain ('Buttermilk Burn'). Climb up this. On the way look for two large boulders; the lower one with an overhang acting as a shelter and the higher one, the 'Narnain Stone', used for rock climbing. From this point climb steeply N beside stream towards summit, finding your way between rocky outcrops, on to the narrow Spearhead Ridge. This leads to flat summit of Beinn Narnain (926m 3036ft TP. BM S5954). Return by going WNW, then swing round to top of Allt a' Bhalachain, then back SE to upward route.

An alternative route upwards avoiding the narrow ridge, is by the suggested return route.

To shorten the walk, return by outward route.

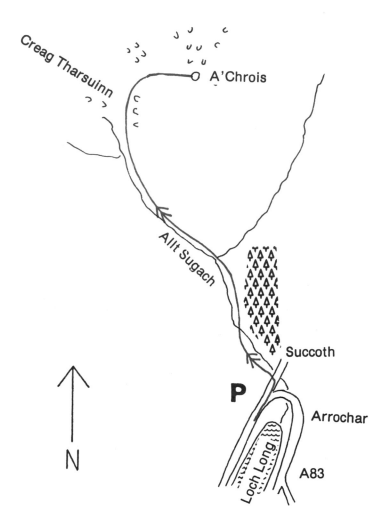

Creag Tharsuinn

A'Chrois

Allt Sugach

Succoth

P

Arrochar

Loch Long

A83

N

WALK 43

43. A 'Chrois (The Cross).

Ordnance Survey map 56. Distance from city centre to car parking: 58.2km 36.2ml. Walking distance from parking: 10.5km 6.5ml. Height of climbing: 839m 2752f. A steep climb to one of the spectacular 'Arrochar Alps', to some people the most attractive of these.

Park car at Succoth road end parking place. NN293049. See walk 41.

Walk N along side road to Succoth 365m 400y, turn left uphill. Follow path on NE side of Allt Sugach up to Creag Tharsuinn, then on to summit of A'Chrois (849m 2785f). Return by same route.

It is not practicable to shorten this walk, except by turning back before completion.

Ben Arthur (The Cobbler). Walk 41.

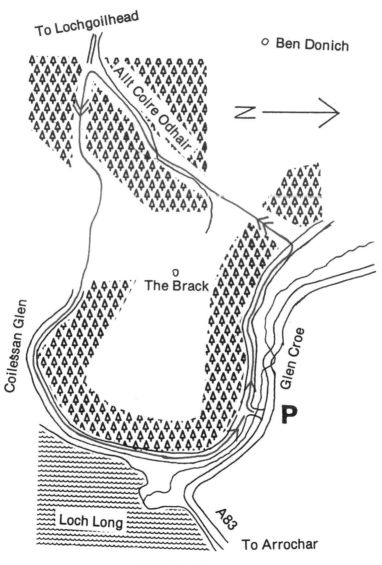

To Lochgoilhead

Ben Donich

Allt Coire Odhair

N

The Brack

Coilessan Glen

Glen Croe

P

Loch Long

A83

To Arrochar

WALK 44

44.   *Coilessan Glen.*

Ordnance Survey map 56. Distance from city centre to car parking: 62.8km 39ml. Walking distance from parking: 20km 12.4ml. Height of climbing: 506m 1660f. A long walk but mostly on paths or forestry roads with changing scenery. Coilessan means 'the wood of the waterfalls', and these can be seen during the steep descent through the glen.

Park car at or near Forestry Commission buildings in Glen Croe. NN255042. To get there follow route as for walk 40, but continue along A83 to Glen Croe. The turn off to the parking place is about 1.5km 0.9ml after the road leaves Loch Long.

Walk W (to the right) along forestry road for 2.3km 1.5ml, then turn left up a marked path through break in forest to bealach between The Brack and Ben Donich. Drop down to path along Allt Coire Odhair and follow this SW keeping on left side of burn. After about 3km 2ml this will join path from Lochgoilhead. Turn E and up along this path which will take you, latterly, down Coilessan Glen. This is a steep descent beside a stream and is an enjoyable change. At the foot the path comes to a forestry road near Loch Long. Proceed NNW along this road to start.

It is not practicable to shorten this route.

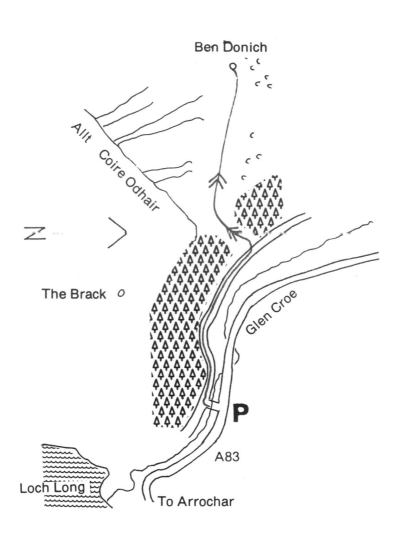

Ben Donich

Allt Coire Odhair

N

The Brack

Glen Croe

P

A83

Loch Long

To Arrochar

WALK 45

45. Ben Donich.

Ordnance Survey map 56. Distance from city centre to car parking: 62.8km 39ml. Walking distance from parking: 15.3km 9.6ml. Height of climbing: 758m 2486f. Quite a steep climb, but gives a great sense of achievement. Known as 'the brown mountain', it is a Corbett.

Park car in Glen Croe. NN255042. See walk 44.

Walk as for walk 44 to the point between The Brack and Ben Donich. At this stage you will have climbed about two-fifths of the way to the top. Strike W up broad, grassy slope to summit of Ben Donich (847m 2774f. TP. BM S8799). Return by same route.

It is not practicable to shorten this walk.

Beinn an Lochain. Walk 47.

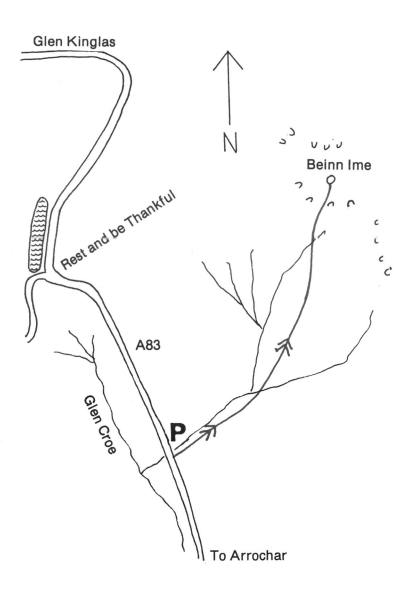

Glen Kinglas

N

Beinn Ime

Rest and be Thankful

A83

Glen Croe

P

To Arrochar

WALK 46

46.   *Beinn Ime.*

Ordnance Survey map 56. Distance from city centre to car parking: 65.3km 40.6ml. Walking distance from parking: 8.4km 5.2ml. Height of climbing: 826m 2709f. A constant steep ascent to the summit of this conical rocky mountain, which is a Munro.

Park car at space on E side of A83 in Glen Croe, about 5km 3ml after leaving Loch Long. NN243060. To get there follow route as for walk 40, but continue along A83 to Glen Croe. There are suitable spaces just before and after a stone bridge over a burn.

Climb steeply on path NE up glen then NNE to summit of Beinn Ime (1011m 3318f. TP. BM 12166). Return by same route.

It is not practicable to shorten this walk.

Beinn Ime. Walk 46.

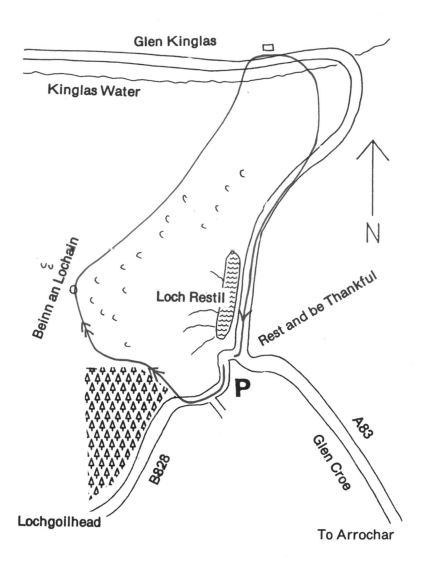

WALK 47

47.   Beinn an Lochain.

Ordnance Survey map 56. Distance from city centre to car parking: 67.6km 42ml. Walking distance from parking: 10.3km 6.4ml. Height of climbing: 766m 2512f. There have been disputes as to whether this is a Munro or not, but it is a wonderful climb. By starting high there is less climbing.

Park car at 'Rest and be Thankful' on A83. NN229074. To get there follow route as for walk 40, but continue along A83 to and up Glen Croe to its summit.

Walk along B828 (Lochgoilhead road) for 0.8km 0.5ml. Just past forestry road going off on the left, and immediately before forestry on right, climb up hill round outside of tree area. Then strike up hill among rocks and along ridge to summit of Beinn an Lochain (920m 3021f). Return by continuing NNE and descending to Glen Kinglas. Turn right (E) and keep on S side of river. Join old road coming across river and follow this S and up until it joins modern road. Either walk up road, or walk along W side of Loch Restil to start.

To shorten the walk, return from Beinn an Lochain by outward route. Save 4.3km 2.7ml.

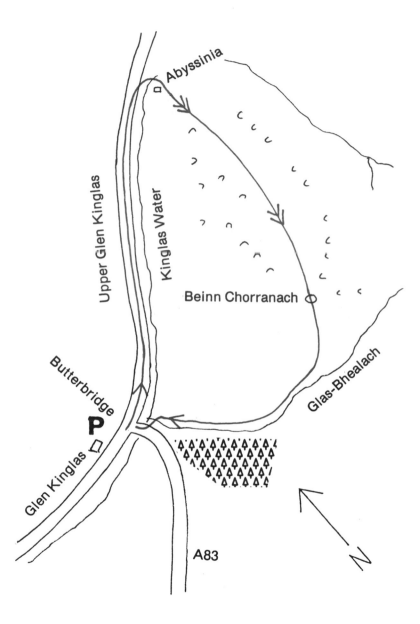

WALK 48

48.   Beinn Chorranach.

Ordnance Survey map 56. Distance from city centre to car parking: 69km 42.9ml. Walking distance from parking: 11.6km 7.2ml. Height of climbing: 655m 2148f. An interesting steep climb in rocky terrain.

Park car at side of A83 ncar Butterbridge in Glen Kinglas. NN235095. To get there, follow route as for walk 40, but continue along A83 to and up Glen Croe, past 'Rest and be Thankful' and down to Glen Kinglas.

Leave main road and walk NE along old road in Upper Glen Kinglas. At Abyssinia (a ruin, named by a former owner who had travelled widely in the country of that name) turn on to mountain and climb up the long stccp shoulder in a S direction to the summit of Beinn Chorranach (885m 2903f). Descend to Glas-Bhealach then down beside the burn to start.

It is not practicable to shorten this walk.

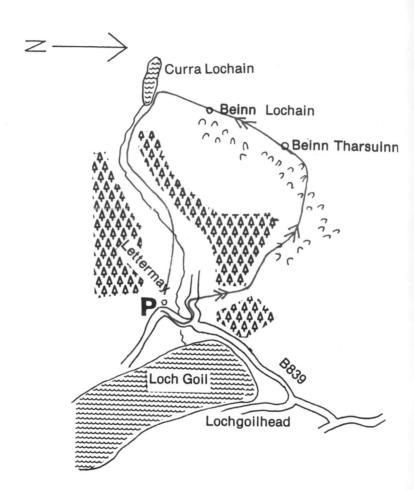

N →

Curra Lochain

Beinn Lochain

Beinn Tharsuinn

Lettermay

P

Loch Goil

B839

Lochgoilhead

WALK 49

49. *Beinn Tharsuinn and Beinn Lochain.*

Ordnance Survey map 56. Distance from city centre to car parking: 76.6km 47.6ml. Walking distance from parking: 12.1km 7.5ml. Height of climbing: 774m 2539f. Very interesting rocky mountains with short walking approach.

Park car near Lettermay, Lochgoilhead. NN188002. To get there, follow route as for walk 40 but continue along A83 to and up Glen Croe. At 'Rest and be Thankful' turn left along B828, then S along B839 to Lochgoilhead. At entrance to village take right fork, signposted 'Carrick Castle', leading to W side of loch and follow through until Lettermay Burn is crossed.

Walk back along road, turn left through farm and up winding road. Look for narrow forest break rising up the hill on the right. Go up this. At the top turn left and walk along gradually climbing up. Then make circular route round the tops to summit of Beinn Tharsuinn (621m 2037f). Continue SSW to Beinn Lochain (703m 2306f).

Descend to Curra Lochain, and turn left along track which leads down to Lettermay.

To shorten the walk, return from Beinn Tharsuinn by outward route. Save 2.3km 1.4ml.

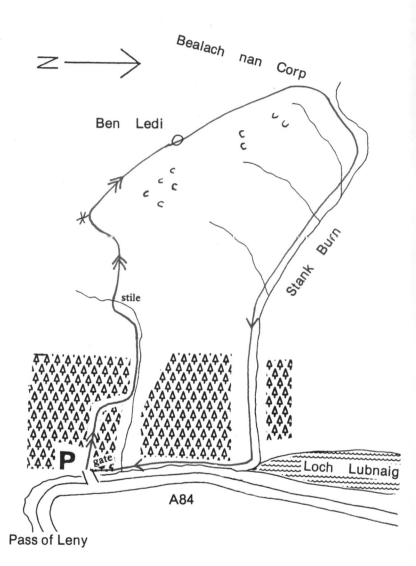

Bealach nan Corp

Ben Ledi

Stank Burn

stile

Loch Lubnaig

P

gate

A84

Pass of Leny

WALK 50

'TWIXT CALLANDER AND CRIANLARICH

50.   Ben Ledi.

Ordnance Survey map 57. Distance from city centre to car parking: 63.4km 39.4ml. Walking distance from parking: 11.6km 7.2ml. Height of climbing: 739m 2424f. A continuous climb to summit of a well-known and well-liked mountain, where lead was once mined. It is called 'the hill of God', or 'the mountain of gentle slope'! and is a Corbett.

Park car in Ben Ledi car park across river bridge at N end of Pass of Leny. NN586093. To get there take A81 (Glasgow to Callander) via Milngavie, Blanefield, Ballat junction, Aberfoyle road junction, Port of Menteith. Turn left at Callander onto A84. After Falls of Leny watch for bridge over river. Go over this and park.

From this point go through gate and follow the steep marked path which has been over used and is, therefore, soft and muddy. Duck boards have been laid at some of the worst parts. After leaving the woodland, there is a burn to cross and a stile over a fence. There is a cairn just before turning up on to the top ridge. There are a few false tops. The route is clear to the summit of Ben Ledi (879m 2883f. TP. BM S6956). Return by going NW along the ridge marked by line of fence posts and

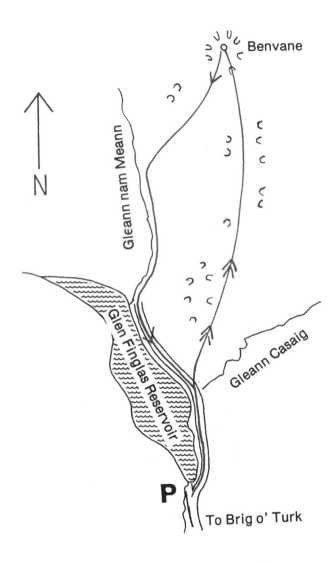

N

Benvane

Gleann nam Meann

Glen Finglas Reservoir

Gleann Casaig

P

To Brig o' Turk

WALK   51

descending to Bealach nan Corp. Turn right and down. Keep Stank Burn on your left. Join forestry road then onto old railway track, and go S along this to start.

To shorten the walk, return from Ben Ledi summit by outward route. Save 4.8km 3ml.

51. Benvane from Glen Finglas.

Ordnance Survey map 57. Distance from city centre to car parking: 55.8km 34.7ml. Walking distance from parking: 18.8km 11.7ml. Height of climbing: 664m 2183f. A very satisfying walk first by water then up onto a broad ridge.

Park car near Glen Finglas Reservoir. NN531075. To get there, take A81 (Glasgow to Callander) via Milngavie, Blanefield, Ballat junction, to Aberfoyle road junction. Then turn left along A821 to Aberfoyle, then turn right up Duke's Pass road (built in 1885 by the Duke of Montrose, and made suitable for motors in 1932). Continue along and down this road to Loch Achray. Turn right at Trossachs along N side of Loch Achray and on to Brig o' Turk village. ('Brig o' Turk' means 'boar's bridge', said to be where the last boar in Scotland was killed). Turn left up Glen Finglas road and proceed to end of public road at entrance to reservoir grounds.

Walk up waterworks road being the right fork where the car is parked. This road will lead you along side of reservoir at a height to enable you to enjoy the view. After about 1.5km 1ml and immediately you cross the river coming down Gleann Casaig, strike up hill keeping to centre of ridge. After 6.4km 4ml and a few false tops this leads to the summit of Benvane (818m 2685f).

Return by dropping gradually down to right (SW) to Allt Gleann nam Meann, and along its side to the reservoir and by track and road to start.

It is not practicable to shorten this walk, except by turning back before reaching the top.

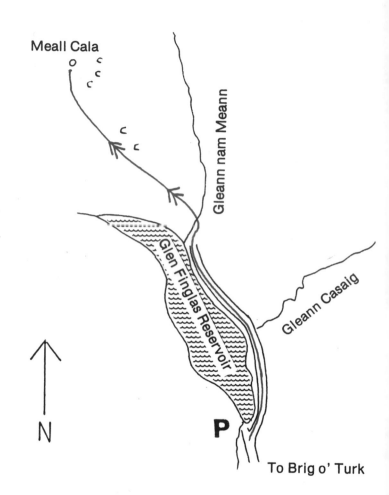

Meall Cala

Gleann nam Meann

Glen Finglas Reservoir

Gleann Casaig

N

P

To Brig o' Turk

WALK   52

52. *Meall Cala.*

Ordnance Survey map 57. Distance from city centre to car parking: 55.8km 34.7ml. Walking distance from parking: 17.2km 10.7ml. Height of climbing 517m 1701f. After walking alongside the reservoir the ascent is to one of the minor tops in a beautiful area.

Park car near Glen Finglas Reservoir. NN531075. See walk 51.

Walk up waterworks road being the right fork where the car is parked. This road will lead you along the side of the reservoir, over the river coming down Gleann Casaig and round to Gleann nam Meann (about 5.2km 3.3ml). Turn up that glen and cross the burn. Climb onto hill, avoiding rocks at early steep part. Then keeping to centre of ridge climb to summit of Meall Cala (674m 2201f). Return by same route.

It is not practicable to shorten this walk, except by turning back before reaching the top.

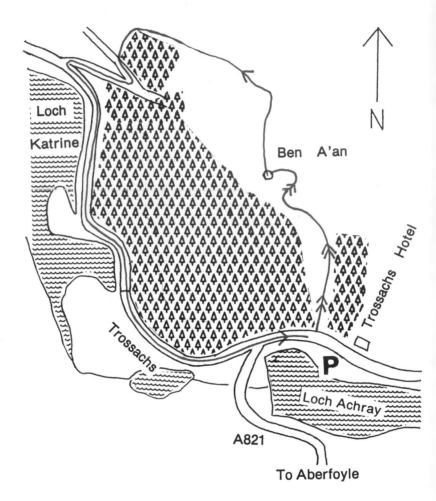

Loch Katrine

Ben A'an

Trossachs Hotel

Trossachs

P

Loch Achray

A821

To Aberfoyle

N

WALK 53

53.   Ben A'an (Binnein).

Ordnance Survey map 57. Distance from city centre to car parking: 53.5km 33.1ml. Walking distance from parking: 11.5km 7.2ml. Height of climbing: 387m 1269f. A sharp, but quite short, climb to a famous viewpoint over the Trossachs. Well-named 'the pinnacle' in Gaelic. It was in 1810 that Sir Walter Scott wrote *'The Lady of the Lake'* which immortalised Loch Katrine and the Trossachs.

Park car at car park on loch side of A821 at W end of Loch Achray. NN510070. To get there, see walk 51, but, after Trossachs road junction, look for car park on right (before Trossachs Hotel).

Cross road to marked path which goes very steeply up through woodland until it emerges not far from top. There is a short, near to level, part of the walk here. Then follow steep, and well-marked, path up and round left to summit of Ben A'an (462m 1520f). Return by descending on W side then across small glen (penetrating easily a high deer fence where it turns at an angle and is joined by a lower fence on its other side) and up and to left along 'slit' in hill. From the top descend still westward along top of woodland and turn down when it ends. This will take you down to a forestry road. Turn left along this road and when it meets another such road turn right. This road continues down some way before it reaches the tarmac loch-side road. Follow along this to left, then public road from pier to start.

To shorten the walk, return from summit of Ben A'an by outward route. Save 6.1km 3.8ml.

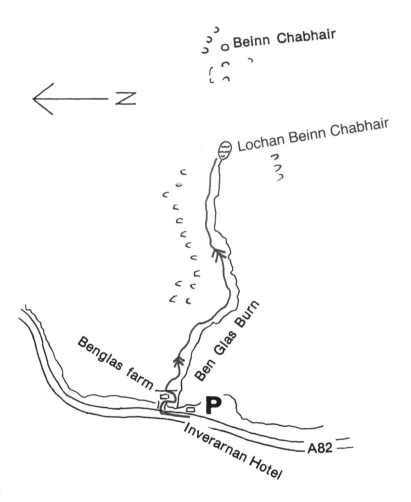

Beinn Chabhair

Lochan Beinn Chabhair

Ben Glas Burn

Benglas farm

P

Inverarnan Hotel

A82

N

WALK 54

54. *Lochan Beinn Chabhair.*

Ordnance Survey map 56. Distance from city centre to car parking: 70.3km 43.7ml. Walking distance from parking: 9.8km 6.1ml. Height of climbing: 580m 1902f. A steep mountain path through rocky terrain to a lochan surrounded by imposing mountains. The route follows the boundary between Strathclyde and Central Regions.

Park car at or near Inverarnan Hotel. NN318184. To get there, go via Anniesland, Bowling, Dumbarton, and A82 (Loch Lomond W side road), continuing 3.6km 2.2ml past head of loch to Inverarnan.

Walk short way up main road, then across bridge over river on right. Turn right along path which winds round field. Go over stile to back of Beinglas farm, but instead of turning right along West Highland Way, turn and find path steeply ascending mountain. This winds its way up near the Ben Glas Burn. After initial steep climb, the route flattens out before another less steep climb to Lochan Beinn Chabhair. A magnificent place on a sunny day to lie on your back for an hour or two. (The very fit can then climb Beinn Chabhair (931m 3053f — Munro) or one of the lesser tops surrounding this lochan.) Return by same route.

It is not practicable to shorten this walk.

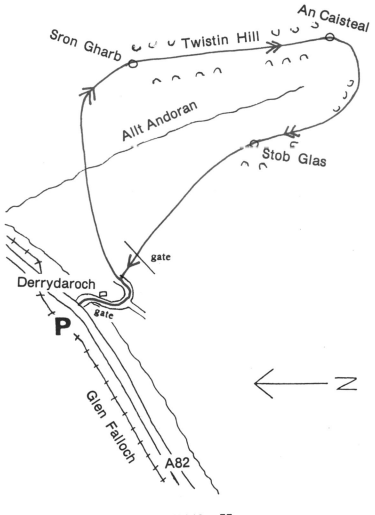

Sron Gharb

An Caisteal

Twistin Hill

Allt Andoran

Stob Glas

gate

Derrydaroch

gate

P

Glen Falloch

A82

WALK 55

55. *An Caisteal (The Castle).*

Ordnance Survey map 50. Distance from city centre to car parking: 75.6km 47ml. Walking distance from parking: 14.2km 8.8ml. Height of climbing: 871m 2857f. A stiff climb after a longish journey, so start early in good weather.

Park car on A82 in Glen Falloch on side-of-road parking place opposite Derrydaroch road entrance. NN352220. To get there, take A82 (Loch Lomond W side road) about 5.3km 3.3ml beyond Inverarnan at N end of loch.

Go through gate, walk down road, cross river by bridge, pass Derrydaroch and proceed SW along rough road. The road then turns uphill. When it divides, go left. When it ends, strike E over hills to lower part of Sron Gharbh. Climb up the ridge to summit (708m 2322f), and along Twistin Hill to An Caisteal summit (995m 3265f). This is a strenuous walk over rough terrain.

Return by going round end of Allt Andoran glen and down ridge to Stob Glas (708m 2322f). (This is very steep with much rock. If in any doubt, return by outward route.) From that top drop down to end of rough road from which you started, passing through a gate in a fence shortly before reaching it.

It is not practicable to shorten this walk, except by turning back before reaching summit of An Caisteal.

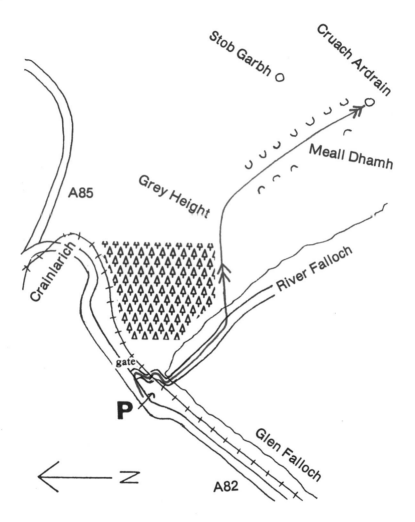

Stob Garbh ○

Cruach Ardrain ○

Meall Dhamh

Grey Height

A85

Crainlarich

River Falloch

gate

P

N

Glen Falloch

A82

WALK 56

56. Cruach Ardrain.

Ordnance Survey maps 50 and 51. Distance from city centre to car parking: 78.5km 48.8ml. Walking distance from parking: 15.1km 9.4ml. Height of climbing: 884m 2900f. Another long hard climb which should be done in good weather, but certainly one to be added to your list of achievements. Its name means 'the high heap', and it is a Munro.

Park car at right (E) side of A82 in Glen Falloch where River Falloch flows from hills to the glen (2.5km 1.6ml before Crianlarich). NN368238. There is a small area suitable for parking at start of straight stretch of road. To get there, take A82 (Loch Lomond W side road) about 8.4km 5.2ml beyond Inverarnan at N end of loch.

Walk from car farther N to a gate. Go over this and follow rough track down to and under railway bridge. Then over bridge across river. Follow road beside river until end of woodland on other side. Cross river and climb to Grey Height. (685m 2247f). Go SSE along ridge to Meall Dhamh (806m 2645f). Continue in same direction by small descent (50m 55f) then steep climb to summit of Cruach Ardrain (1045m 3428f). Before the top there are two small cairns, and at the top a large cairn. Return by same route. An alternative return route is by Stob Garbh (957m 3148f) and down ridge to forest. Look for firebreak which will lead you through to railway line. Turn left down to start.

To shorten the walk, turn back at Meall Dhamh. Save 3.3km 2.1ml.

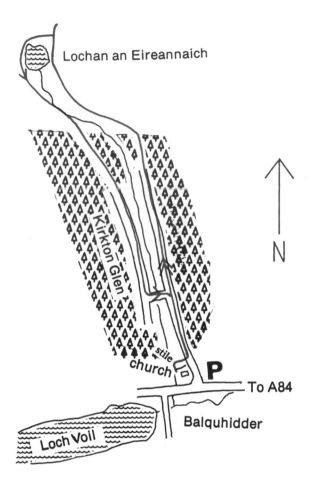

Lochan an Eireannaich

Kirkton Glen

N

stile

church

P

To A84

Balquhidder

Loch Voil

WALK 57

57. *Lochan an Eireannaich (Kirkton Glen).*

Ordnance Survey map 51. Distance from city centre to car parking: 78.8km 49ml. Walking distance from parking: 12.2km 7.6ml. Height of climbing: 446m 1463f. A path and forest walk being one part of a right-of-way through to Glen Dochart. Quite easy. Note Rob Roy's grave in churchyard before you start the walk. It was Wordsworth who said "The eagle he was lord above, and Rob was lord below".

Park car at Balquhidder. NN535209. To get there, go via Callander (see walk 50), but continue N on A84 through Strathyre turning left at Kingshouse Hotel along Balquhidder road.

Find path leading out of churchyard at back of church (NW corner). Follow this along burn, then sharp right turn, up and over a stile. The path goes up Kirkton Glen through woodland (keep the burn on your left), finally emerging shortly before Lochan an Eireannaich (The Little Loch of the Irishman) (578m 1896f). Continue through gap in fence and then a little round to right to see the view. Retrace steps to lochan and return on other side of burn by going through woodland (takes a bit of exploring) and joining forestry road which, after about 3km 2ml, crosses the burn to join path which you came up. And so to start.

It is not practicable to shorten this walk, except by turning back before the end.

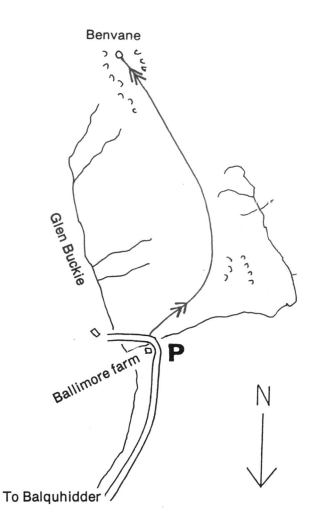

Benvane

Glen Buckie

Ballimore farm

P

To Balquhidder

N

WALK 58

58. Benvane (Loch Lubnaig).

Ordnance Survey map 57. Distance from city centre to car parking: 83km 51.6ml. Walking distance from parking: 12.2km 7.6ml. Height of climbing: 603m 1978f. An easy, pleasant climb after rather a long car journey. The origin of the name is thought to be either 'mountain of the river' or 'the white peak'.

Park car at Ballimore farm. NN530175. (See walk 57). Turn S at Balquhidder to Ballimore.

Start walk by crossing bridge over burn, then go SSW up hill then SSE along ridge to summit of Benvane (818m 2685f), which is a Corbett. This is a straightforward walk with no problems. Return by same route.

It is not practicable to shorten this walk, except by returning before reaching the top.

Cruach Ardrain. Walk 56.

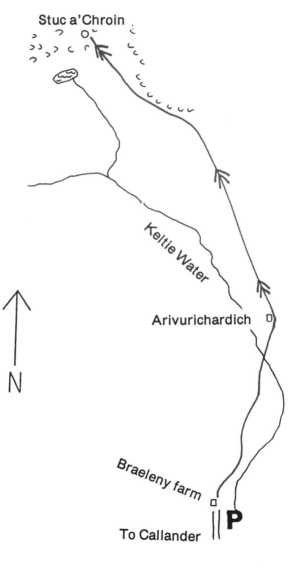

Stuc a'Chroin

Keltie Water

Arivurichardich

N

Braeleny farm

To Callander

P

WALK 59

'TWIXT CALLANDER AND COMRIE

59. Stuc a' Chroin.

Ordnance Survey map 57. Distance from city centre to car parking: 62.1km 38.6ml. Walking distance from parking: 21km 13ml. Height of climbing: 741m 2430f. A long, hard day but exhilarating. An area of rocky peaks. The name means 'a peak like a horn or cloven foot', and it is a Munro.

Park car at Braeleny farm, N of Callander. NN637111. To get there see walk 50 (to Callander), then Bracklinn Falls road (off SE end of main street), taking left fork from that road, only at car park for the falls. Braeleny farm is then about 2km 1.2ml farther on.

Continue on foot along road and path, crossing Keltie Water at ford and, at Arivurichardich bothy, forking left along indistinct path gradually uphill to ridge. (Do not follow the path as it turns right over the pass). Climb steadily over this long rock-strewn ridge to the flat summit of Stuc a' Chroin (972m 3189f. Two cairns). This ridge is part of the Central/Tayside Regional boundary. The route from Braelany to Arivurichardich is a right of way. Return by same route.

It is not practicable to shorten this walk, except by returning before reaching the summit.

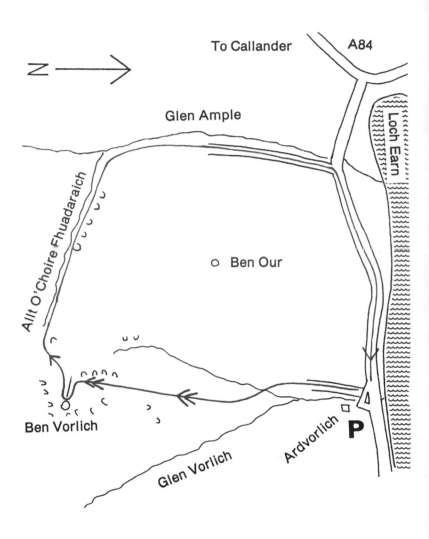

N →

To Callander   A84

Glen Ample

Loch Earn

Allt O'Choire Fhuadaraich

○ Ben Our

Ben Vorlich

Glen Vorlich   Ardvorlich   P

WALK 60

60. Ben Vorlich (Loch Earn).

Ordnance Survey maps 51 and 57. Distance from city centre to car parking: 83.7km 52ml. Walking distance from parking: 21.4km 13.3ml. Height of climbing: 861m 2824f. A long and a stiff climb, but certainly worth doing, especially since it is a Munro. The name of the mountain means 'peak of the sea-bag'.

Park car near Ardvorlich on Loch Earn. NN632229. To get there, see walk 50 (to Callander), then NNW along A84 to about 1km 0.6ml before Lochearnhead. Turn right along road on S side of the loch for about 3km 1.9ml.

Start through east gate of Ardvorlich House along private road and continue along track up Glen Vorlich striking up the mountain after about 1.6km 1ml. The top is steep and there is rock in plenty around. An old fence going E is followed to the summit of Ben Vorlich (985m 3231f. TP. BM S6931. There is a cairn at the SE end). Return by descending WNW alongside Allt O' Choire Fhuadaraich to Glen Ample. Here a path, then a road, takes you down to lochside road. Turn right and back to car.

To shorten the walk, return from summit of Ben Vorlich by outward route. Save 7.8km 4.8ml.

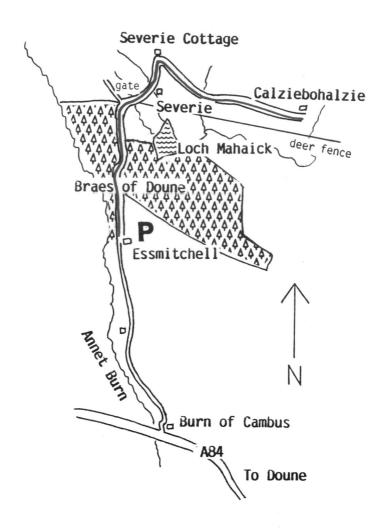

Severie Cottage

gate

Severie

Calziebohalzie

deer fence

Loch Mahaick

Braes of Doune

P

Essmitchell

N

Annet Burn

Burn of Cambus

A84

To Doune

WALK 61

61. *Braes of Doune.*

Ordnance Survey map 57. Distance from city centre to car parking: 61km 37.2ml. Walking distance from parking: 12km 7.5ml. Height of climbing: 115m 377f. A short pleasant walk in open country.

Park car at Essmitchell. NN701056. To get there take M90 and M9 (Glasgow to Dunblane), leaving at junction 10. Turn left along A84 to Doune, then continue for 2.1km 1.2ml and turn right along minor road just before Annet Burn. Go up this for 2.8km 1.3ml to Essmitchell. Car parking is very restricted here. It may be necessary to return down road to suitable place.

Walk along road N between trees. At Y junction go right, passing Severie (named Coldhome on some maps) to Severie Cottage (or named Severie). Continue along road to Calziebohalzie. Return by same route. It was previously possible to walk round the S side of Loch Mahaick but a high deer fence has been erected which makes this almost impossible.

It is not practicable to shorten this walk.

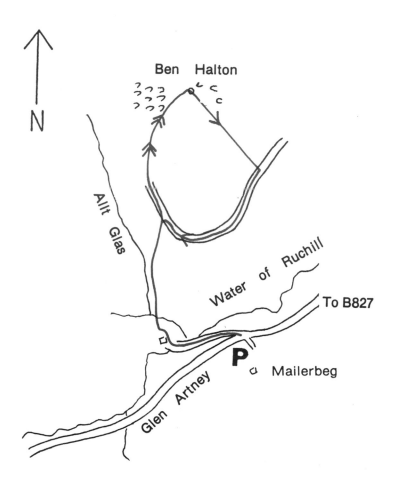

Ben Halton

N

Allt Glas

Water of Ruchill

To B827

P

Mailerbeg

Glen Artney

WALK 62

62. Ben Halton.

Ordnance Survey map 57. Distance from city centre to car parking: 78.4km 48.7ml. Walking distance from parking: 13.5km 8.4ml. Height of climbing: 451m 1484f. A pleasant little climb in a different setting. It is in Tayside Region.

Park car near Mailerbeg. NN729173. To get there take M80 and M9 (Glasgow to Dunblane) to its end, then through Dunblane. Turn left along A822 at Greenloaning. Turn left along B827 just past Braco. After 10.5km 6.5ml turn left along road which leads into Glen Artney. 5km 3.1ml along this is Mailerbeg.

Walk down an old road on right which goes forward at an angle down to the river (Water of Ruchill). Cross bridge and go N, crossing tributary. Continue N up glen of Allt Glas, but strike on to hill on right to join hill road. Follow this N to its end then strike up to summit of Ben Halton (620m 2034f). If the weather suits, relax here and have your lunch.

Return by dropping down SE to join hill road round to where you joined it earlier, and so back to car.

It is not practicable to shorten this walk.

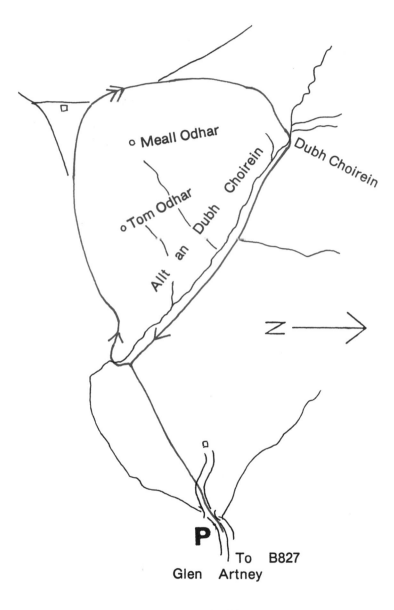

o Meall Odhar

Dubh Choirein

o Tom Odhar

Allt an Dubh Choirein

N ⟶

P

To B827

Glen Artney

WALK 63

63. Head of Glen Artney.

Ordnance Survey map 57. Distance from city centre to car parking: 81.9km 50.9ml. Walking distance from parking: 22.5km 14ml. Height of climbing: 426m 1400f. A walk along some old routes in a remote mountain area, in the Tayside Region.

Park car at end of road along Glen Artney. NN698157. To get there take M80 and M9 (Glasgow to Dunblane) to its end, then through Dunblane. Turn left along A822 at Greenloaning. Turn left along B827 just past Braco. After 10.5km 6.5ml turn left along road which leads into Glen Artney. Go to end, just before bridge crosses Water of Ruchill.

Walk across bridge and follow track SW, and after about 3km 1.9ml cross Allt an Dubh Choirein. Pass below Tom Odhar. Instead of following path down to ford, swing round to right below Meall Odhar and join other path coming up from ford. This path now runs across the side of the hill and divides. Take the right fork which leads through a bealach (Ben Vorlich stands ahead of you) and down to meet a path from the N (Loch Earn) at Dubh Choirein. Turn right and go down glen to meet path which you came along earlier. Turn left along to car.

To shorten the walk, return from position below Meall Odhar by outward route. Save 6km 3.7ml.

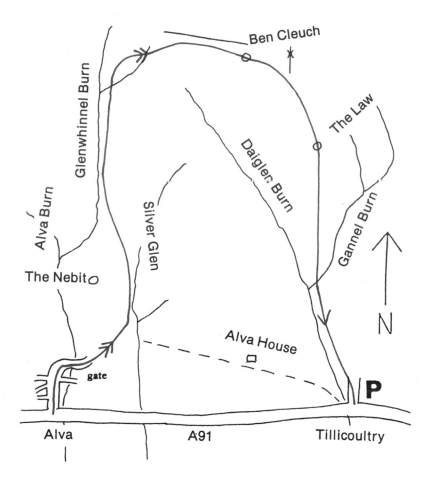

WALK   64

OCHIL HILLS

64.   Ben Cleuch.

Ordnance Survey map 58. Distance from city centre to car parking: 62.1km 38.6ml. Walking distance from parking: 14.2km 8.8ml. Height of climbing: 709m 2326f. Not difficult but quite long climb, with interesting start and finish.

Park car in car park E side of Tillicoultry on A91 (Stirling to Cupar) at Tourist Centre. NS914971. To get there go by A80 and M80 (Glasgow to Stirling), continuing on M9 to junction 10. Leave motorway and join A84 turning right at roundabout along A84, then A9 and over River Forth. At Causewayhead roundabout, go straight across on to minor road and then turn right onto B998 which joins A91. Follow this to Tillicoultry.

Take local bus back to Alva. Walk up Brook Street to the N, then up by Alva Burn. At waterworks take right fork and go through pedestrians-only gate. This leads to path going up and across face of hill, The Nebit, to right. You will then be in Silver Glen. (Alternatively, walk from car park at Tillicoultry past golf course on your left and Alva House stables on your right, by track, joining Silver Glen path above Alva.) Follow the path up the glen and at its head swing right and round to Ben Cleuch ridge, and so along fence to summit (720m 2363f.TP. BM S1605. Indicator). Sometimes this hill is called Glenwhappen Rig. There are two cairns on top. Return

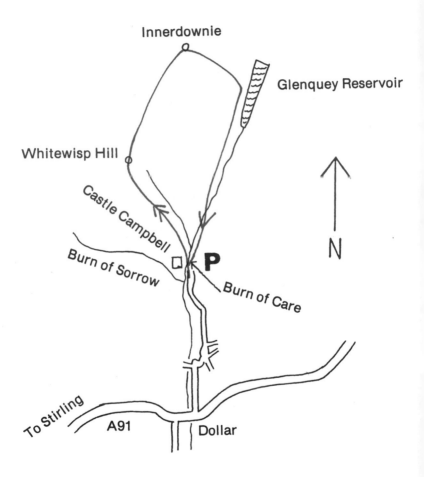

Innerdownie

Glenquey Reservoir

Whitewisp Hill

Castle Campbell

Burn of Sorrow

P

Burn of Care

N

To Stirling

A91

Dollar

WALK 65

by continuing along ridge past radio mast and via The Law (638m 2094f) down to junction of Gannel Burn and Daiglen Burn. Cross the former and follow the path down to Tillicoultry.

It is not practicable to shorten this walk.

65. *Whitewisp Hill and Innerdownie.*

Ordnance Survey map 58. Distance from city centre to car parking: 69.3km 43.1ml. Walking distance from parking: 12.7km 7.9ml. Height of climbing: 491m 1610f. An easier Ochil Hills walk, with an opportunity to see Dollar Glen if you wish.

Park car in car park at top of Castle Campbell road, Dollar. NS962994. To get there see walk 64, but continue past Tillicoultry to Dollar, then turn left up road on far side of river. Follow signs for Castle Campbell. The castle was built in the 15th century, and was originally called 'Castle Gloume'. It was taken over by Colin Campbell, 1st Earl of Argyll, in 1489. What is left of it is now looked after by the Historic Buildings and Monuments Department of the Scottish Office.

Walk up path beside Burn of Care (the Burn of Sorrow is on the other side of the castle), but crossing burn before it divides. Carry on up to summit of Whitewisp Hill (643m 2110f). Strike NNE by dyke to Innerdownie (611m 2004f). Return by dropping down to Glenquey Reservoir, and turning right along path to start.

To shorten the walk, return from Whitewisp Hill by outward route. Save 6.1km 3.8ml.

An interesting addition to the walk would be for you to leave your car in Dollar and walk up the glen. This is looked after by the National Trust for Scotland and is spectacular.

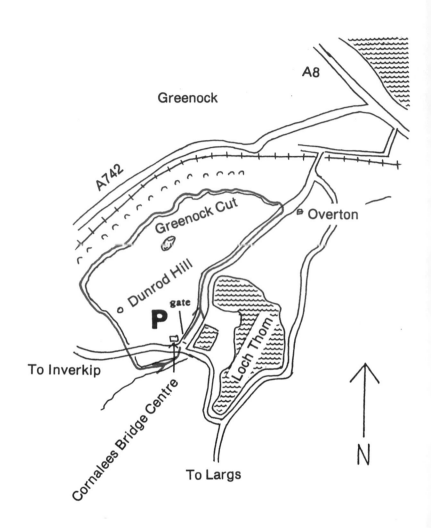

WALK 66

INVERCLYDE, CUNNINGHAME AND RENFREW

66.   The Greenock Cut.

Ordnance Survey map 63. Distance from city centre to car parking: 45.9km 28.5ml. Walking distance from parking: 15.1km 9.4ml. Height of climbing: 15m 49f. A relaxing level walk on grass path high above the Firth of Clyde.

Park car at Cornalees Bridge Centre car park. NS248722. To get there, take M8 and A8 to Greenock then, at fire station, turn left along Dellingburn Street then Largs Road, which goes straight up the hill. At the top the road turns right and becomes 'Drumfrochar Road'. Continue on this until you turn off on left along 'Loch Thom Road' and later 'Old Largs Road'. Do not go along the road signposted 'To the Cut'. The road goes over moorland and then round Loch Thom. When at the end of that loch (hidden by trees), turn right along Inverkip road (signposted).

Walk along rough road NNE, past Loch Thom Cottage. Join the Greenock Cut (an open cutting built in 1827 by Robert Thom and which was used to supply water to Greenock   superseded in 1973 and is now an ancient monument) near and to the left of Overton. There is a fine pathway along the side of the Cut all the way round to Cornalees. The view over the Firth of Clyde is excellent. Just before the end, look down on river which is rather attractive, especially when in spate.

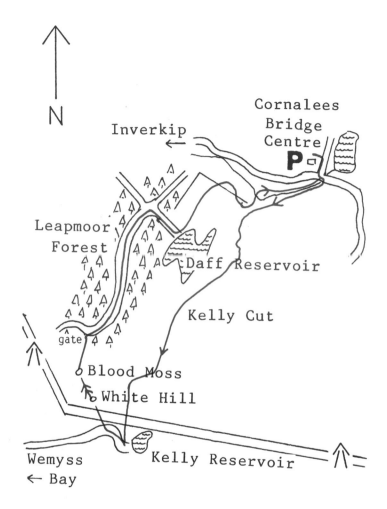

WALK 67

A nature trail leads down to and across it from the Cut walk. As a diversion, Dunrod Hill (298m 977f. TP. BM S5012) can be climbed.

It is not practicable to shorten this walk.

67. *The Kelly Cut.*

Ordnance Survey map 63. Distance from city centre to car parking: 45.9km 28.5ml. Walking distance from parking: 15.6km 9.7ml. Height of climbing: 80m 262f. A less known 'cut' walk with a forest track included.

Park car at Cornalees Bridge Centre car park. NS248722. See walk 66.

Walk back along road a short distance, go over bridge and leave road on right to join Kelly Cut and end of trail path. (The Kelly Cut carried water to the reservoir feeding the Greenock Cut). Instead of following trail down into valley, continue along side of cutting. Eventually you will reach Kelly reservoir. Return NW along reservoir road, then strike off on right and go via White Hill (217m 713f) and Blood Moss (214m 703f. TP. BM S8861) then along remains of old road through gate into Leapmoor forest. Turn right along forestry road, and follow this for some distance. At T junction turn hard right up to Daff Reservoir. Cut over fields ENE keeping wall on left in sight, until reaching fence and wall across route. Cross this to easier walking ground and follow it down to right. When the woodland is reached, walk down between wall and fence, over small wood connecting fence, and steeply down to trail path. Turn left along this, immediately going over stile. Follow trail up to Greenock Cut path and follow this up to Cornalees.

To shorten this walk, return from Kelly Reservoir by outward route. Save 2.4km 1.5ml.

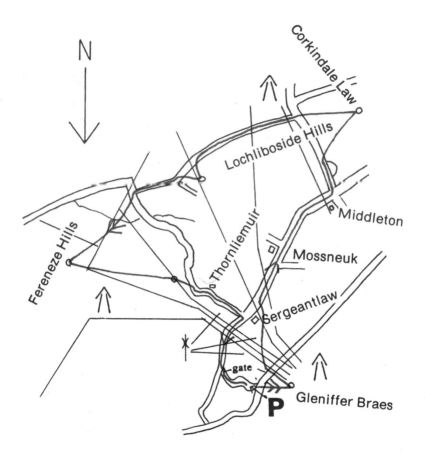

N

Corkindale Law

Lochliboside Hills

Middleton

Ferneze Hills

Thornliemuir

Mossneuk

Sergeantlaw

gate

P Gleniffer Braes

WALK 68

68. Gleniffer Braes, Lochliboside Hills and Fereneze Hills.

Ordnance Survey map 64. Distance from city centre to car parking: 17.1km 10.6ml. Walking distance from parking: 19.1km 11.9ml. Height of climbing: 223m 731f. Starting with far-ranging view over the Clyde valley, followed by easy walking in pleasant countryside. Sometimes on quiet roads, occasionally over wet ground, it provides a relaxation from more strenuous outings.

Park car in Gleniffer Braes car park. NS454604. To get there, go by A8 to Paisley, turning left round 'Paisley Ring Road'. Leave on left along road (Maxwellton Road) signposted 'Irvine'. Follow this sign. Do not turn off at sign 'Gleniffer Braes Park', but after it look for entrance to car park on left (no sign). Go in. It is a very large parking place, situated superbly for a view over the valley.

Walk back to entrance to car park. Cross the road and go through gate. Take left track up to high point — look back on the view. Continue to single pylon on the right which is the summit of Gleniffer Braes (218m 715f. TP. BM S3938). The view from here is spoiled by the pylons and overhead electric lines. Leave this top to the SE down a path skirting woodland (area of grid electric line junctions to the right) through a gate to road. Cross the road and go through another gate. Follow the pylons and fence ahead. Note the two television masts, one on each side of the triple line of pylons. Keeping to the right, go through a gate in dyke and walk over to the right of television mast. After passing Sergeantlaw, go over and join road.

Turn right along road. Pass side road on right, then one on left at Mossneuk farm. Continue on road up hill to crossroads at Middleton farm. Turn left. At the end of the first woodland on right, go through gate and head overland in a SW direction. After crossing a fence you will soon reach Corkindale Law (259m 850f. TP. BM S3579) the highest point on the Lochliboside Hills.

Leave that top in an E direction, and go through a gate in a dyke. Gradually walk downhill to a gate onto a road (a pylon on the other side of the road — this overhead line is not marked on some OS maps). Turn right down the road, then left up the next road. Pass the entrance to the 'Ailsa View Caravan Park' on the left, and a farm on the right. Then, immediately past a small woodland on the left, look for dyke going from the back of that woodland, in which is a TP (211m 692f. BM S3632). Go through a gate and over to it. Then cross field below overhead line, and go through next woodland and out onto road through a gate. Continue along road which goes downhill. On the right, across the valley, is the village of Neilston.

At the foot of the hill, the road turns right, with a minor road coming in on the left. Leave the road, going up beside a row of trees a little to the left. Follow the line of pylons, crossing a stream and some fences, to summit of Fereneze Hills (221m 725f) which is a little to the right. This is not marked; there is an outcrop of rock. Walk across to pylon where the overhead line turns at right angles. Follow this line, but veer west to a dyke at high point where another overhead line comes from the left. Go through a small gate to summit (237m 777f. TP. BM S3619). Go back through gate, turn left down side of dyke to rough road. Turn right along it past Thornliemuir to road near Sergeantlaw. Turn right and follow this, passing a road on left with a gate, then entering Country Walk path (a tarmac path, not signposted). Go along this path, passing an indicator, to car park.

To shorten the walk, omit the summit of Fereneze Hills by going along minor road to Thornliemuir. Save 2.6km 1.6ml.

Ben Vorlich from Meall an t-Seallaidh. Walk 60.

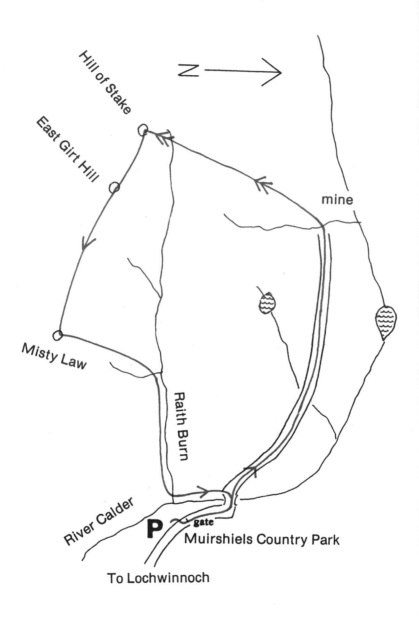

Hill of Stake

East Girt Hill

N →

mine

Misty Law

Raith Burn

River Calder

P

gate

Muirshiels Country Park

To Lochwinnoch

WALK 69

69. *Hill of Stake and Misty Law*

Ordnance Survey map 63. Distance from city centre to car parking: 35.2km 21.9ml. Walking distance from parking: 15.6km 9.7ml. Height of climbing: 351m 1151f. A roughish moorland walk with plenty of fresh air. Not suitable on misty days.

Park car at Muirshiels Country Park car park, which was opened in 1970. NS313632. To get there, go via A737 and A760 Paisley and Johnstone to Lochwinnoch. Then go N on B786 through Lochwinnoch for about 1.7km 1.1ml, then take left fork at white cottage along road signposted 'Muirshiel Country Park' for about 5.4km 3.4ml.

Leave car park and turn left, through gate, along track road, crossing bridge (first bridge has collapsed though crossable on foot, but better to go farther to second and new bridge). Follow this road to old barytes mine (worked from about 1850 to 1969) then turn SSW and climb over heathery rough ground to summit of Hill of Stake (522m 1712f. TP. BM S1576. Cairn). This is the highest point on the watershed between Inverclyde, Renfrew and Cunninghame Districts, and is an excellent viewpoint. Then go SE along boundary via East Girt Hill to Misty Law (507m 1662f). Return by going N to Raith Burn and along its bank until you can cross. After heavy rain this can prove difficult without getting one's feet wet, but as it is near the end of the walk it matters little. Then make for bridge over River Calder which you crossed at start.

It is not practicable to shorten this walk.

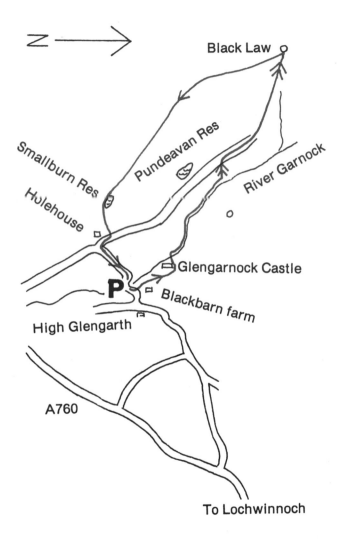

N →

Black Law

Smallburn Res

Pundeavan Res

Holehouse

River Garnock

Glengarnock Castle

P

Blackbarn farm

High Glengarth

A760

To Lochwinnoch

WALK 70

70. *Glengarnock Castle and Black Law.*

Ordnance Survey map 63. Distance from city centre to car parking: 32km 19.9ml. Walking distance from parking: 16.6km 10.3ml. Height of climbing: 382m 1253f. A most interesting walk from farming land to high moorland.

Park car in side road between High Glengarth and Holehouse farms, at Blackbarn farm road end. NS316568. To get there, take A737 then A760 to Lochwinnoch. Then take road on right, 630m 700y out of village, marked 'Glenlora'. Follow this round until High Glengarth, then turn right.

Walk N past Blackbarn farm. When Glengarnock Castle ruins are in sight, veer left over to them. This castle was built in early 1400s for the Riddel family, but was owned by the Cunninghams from mid 1400s to early 1600s. After it was vacated, much of the stone was used to build farm houses, and a storm in 1839 blew down the wall of the keep which is now missing. After looking through the ruin, find and descend steep path to River Garnock. Cross river and follow upstream until opposite Burnt Hill. Climb up on left to old road above Pundeavon Reservoir. Turn right along this road, then ascend Black Law (465m 1525f). Return along hills to SSE, making for Smallburn Reservoir, and joining reservoir road above Holehouse farm. Go through farm and along road to car.

To shorten the walk, turn left (instead of right) along road above Pundeavon reservoir and follow it down to Holehouse. Save 7.1km 4.4ml.

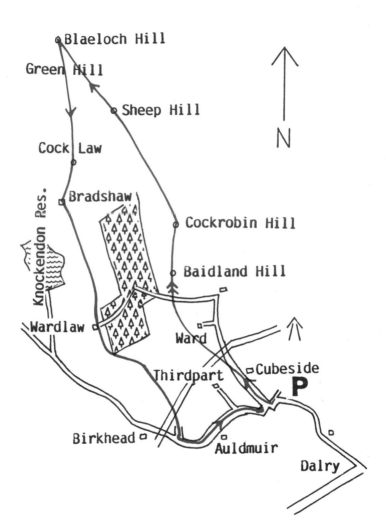

WALK 71

71. *Baidland Hill and Blaeloch Hill.*

Ordnance Survey map 63. Distance from city centre to car parking: 39.4km 24.5ml. Walking distance from parking: 20.2km 12.4ml. Height of climbing: 326m 1069f. A pleasant and easy walk on the open country of Cunninghame hills.

Park car a little NW of Dalry, on road between Broadlie House and Auldmuir at junction with minor road to farm on right. NS272504. To get there take A737 via Paisley and Beith to Dalry. In that town follow signs for West Kilbride to cemetery, and turn right there. Follow signs for Fairlie which takes you past Broadlie House.

Walk up road towards Cubeside, then cut across to left to track above Thirdpart. Follow this up past Ward to summit of Baidland Hill (336m 1097f. TP. BM S4817). Continue the slow climb over Cockrobin Hill and Sheep Hill to Blaeloch Hill (406m 1331f). Note the small Blae Loch just past the top.

Return down via Green Hill and Cock Law to route coming from Fairlie. Join it at Bradshaw (a ruin). This route goes along hillside above Knockendon Reservoir. It is necessary to skirt the young forestry and re-join track at Wardlaw. It reaches moor road near Birkhead. Turn left along road and so back to car.

To shorten the walk, return from Sheep Hill by outward route. Save 6km 3.7ml.

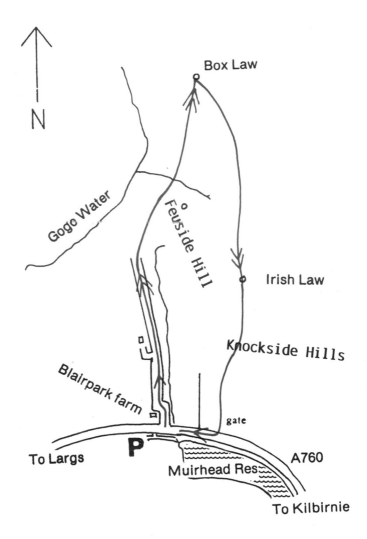

Box Law

Gogo Water

Feuside Hill

Irish Law

Knockside Hills

Blairpark farm

gate

P

To Largs

A760

Muirhead Res.

To Kilbirnie

WALK 72

72. *Box Law and Irish Law.*

Ordnance Survey map 63. Distance from city centre to car parking: 42.2km 26.2ml. Walking distance from parking: 12.2km 7.6ml. Height of climbing 420m 1378f. Pleasant hill walking with no steep ascents. Starts and ends easily, thereafter heathery, tufty and peaty at parts.

Park car on or near old road opposite Blairpark farm on A760 (Kilbirnie to Largs) road, just past Muirhead Reservoir. NS250574. To get there take A737 and A760 to Lochwinnoch, then continue through Kilbirnie.

Cross road and walk along old track round farm. This leads pleasantly uphill. (There is a building higher up on the left with a track up to it.) Continue N until track begins to descend. Turn right and cross over to side of Feuside Hill. Go round its left side and then on to Box Law (470m 1543f). Return direct S to Irish Law (484m 1587f. TP. BM S4822), then over Knockside Hills to main motor road near start.

To shorten this walk, from the point where the track begins to descend, turn right (E), cross over burn and climb Irish Law (omitting Box Law). Save 4.5km 2.8ml.

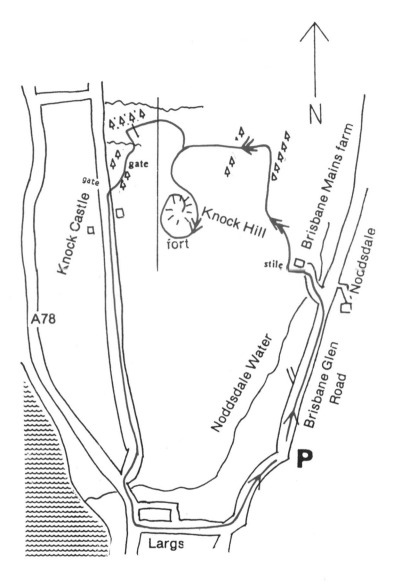

N

Knock Castle

gate

gate

A78

Knock Hill

fort

Knock Castle

Brisbane Mains farm

stile

Noddsdale

Noddsdale Water

Brisbane Glen Road

P

Largs

WALK   73

73. Knock Hill.

Ordnance Survey map 63. Distance from city centre to car parking: 48.8km 30.3ml. Walking distance from parking: 13.4km 8.3ml. Height of climbing: 216m 712f. Quite a short walk, but interesting and a wonderful view from the top over the Firth of Clyde.

Park car at end of houses in Brisbane Glen Road, Largs. NS208605. To get there take A737 via Paisley and Elderslie, and A760 via Lochwinnoch and Kilbirnie to Largs. Pass through to end of town and at the end of esplanade turn right up Douglas Street, which becomes Brisbane Glen Road.

Walk along Brisbane Glen Road, passing entrance to Brisbane Lodge, to road on left marked 'Brisbane Mains'. Go down this and turn with it over a bridge across Noddsdale Water. This leads up to Brisbane Mains farm. Follow road past its front, then over stile at gate, and along side of farm buildings. Continue along line of road and over three more gates, latterly along line of trees on right. When road turns towards the right, cut to left and up through long grass (signs of the old road here). This cuts through line of trees and contours round, then up to base of hill. Avoid taking narrow sheep path up hill to right. Continue on what was old road which becomes a grassy path which spirals clockwise right to the top of Knock Hill (217m 712f. TP. BM S4812). It is quite clear to see that this was once a fort – it is thought to have been occupied by the Picts and, at times, by the Romans. It is said to be a vitrified fort, i.e. where loose stones of the walls were fused together under intense heat, applied by burning timber covering in a strong wind.

Descend on N side steeply to old road which you came up and follow this until it turns away to the right. Walk over rough ground at an angle towards wall on left. At a low part there is an old metal gate in the wall. Go through this. Follow remains of old road, turning slightly left along line of trees. The old road goes along side of trees, through a gateway, and shortly after leaves the trees and turns left. Follow this old track until it crosses burn beside some bushes, then

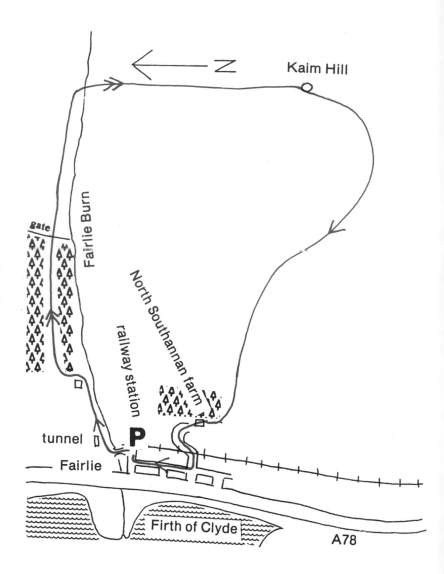

Kaim Hill

Fairlie Burn

gate

North Southannan farm

railway station

tunnel

Fairlie

P

Firth of Clyde

A78

WALK   74

bear right along track to gate, then to another gate on public road near North Lodge of Knock Castle. Walk on twisting road which joins main road just before crossing Noddsdale Water. (At this point note the premises, Netherhall, which were once the home of Lord Kelvin.) After crossing bridge turn second left. This leads to Brisbane Glen Road, and so to car.

To shorten this walk, descend from summit due W across fields to gate on public road. Save 0.9km 0.6ml.

74. Kaim Hill.

Ordnance Survey map 63. Distance from city centre to car parking: 51.6km 32.1ml. Walking distance from parking: 8.8km 5.5ml. Height of climbing: 387m 1269f. A short walk, moderate climbing, and marvellous view over the Firth of Clyde.

Park car at Fairlie railway station. NS210547. To get there see walk 72 but continue to A78 at Largs, turn left at foot of Haylie Brae, go along A78 for about 3km 2ml to Fairlie, and left up Station Road.

Walk along path from station yard over Fairlie Burn and immediately turn right in front of cottages. Follow this path up, alongside burn, past ruins of Fairlie Castle. This castle was owned by the Fairlie family from the 1300s or earlier, and was sold to the Earl of Glasgow about 1700. Continue up old road, then through trees, until wall with gate at end of woodland. Continue up until it is convenient to cross burn on right. Do so and climb to summit of Kaim Hill (387m 1272f. TP. BM S4818). Admire the wonderful view. Return SW off the top, then N to North Southannan farm (on the way look for a place where millstones were hewn out of the rockface). Follow farm road under railway, turn right along street with bungalows, to car.

It is not practicable to shorten this route.

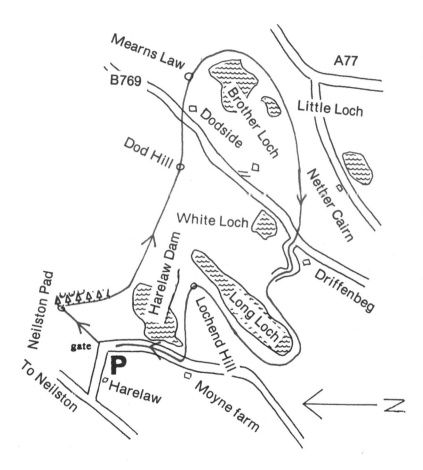

Mearns Law

B769

Dod Hill

Neilston Pad

To Neilston

gate

P

Harelaw

Harelaw Dam

White Loch

Dodside

Brother Loch

Little Loch

A77

Nether Cairn

Driffenbeg

Long Loch

Lochend Hill

Moyne farm

WALK 75

THE SOUTH SIDE

75.   *Neilston Pad and the Five Lochs.*

Ordnance Survey map 64. Distance from city centre to car parking: 19.3km 12ml. Walking distance from parking: 19.5km 12.1ml. Height of climbing: 130m 426f. Combining a walk to a hill prominent when viewed from over the Clyde valley, with some of the many small lochs in the area.

Park car at bend on road between Harelaw farm and Harelaw Dam. NS472545. To get there go to Neilston (on road off A736 at S end of Barrhead) and take road leaving main street opposite church, which goes to E side of railway station. Follow this for 2.6km 1.6ml, then turn left (there is an orange-topped gas pipe line sign just before turn off).

There are three field gates at this bend. Go over the centre one and head up hill NNE towards trees. This will take you to the top of Neilston Pad (258m 850f). After noting the view, return S but walking over to the E side of Harelaw Dam. Then due E to Dod Hill and down to B769 at Dodside. Cross the road and climb Mearns Law (239m 784f). Walk S along E sides of Brother Loch and Little Loch, and curving round below Nether Cairn to B769 where the side road from Driffenbeg meets it. See the White Loch to the right. Go up this side road and down to Long Loch. Walk round the S end of the loch and up the W side of Lochend Hill. Then go W along S

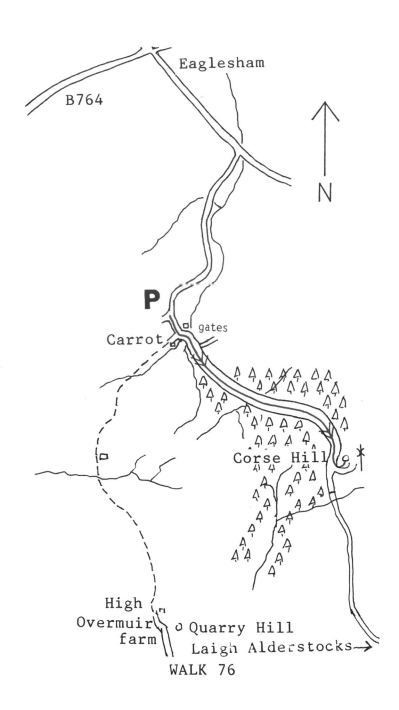

Eaglesham

B764

N

P

Carrot

gates

Corse Hill

High
Overmuir
farm

Quarry Hill

Laigh Alderstocks →

WALK 76

side of Harelaw Dam to come on to road near Moyne farm. From there it is only a short distance to the car.

To shorten the walk, instead of going to Dod Hill, turn S along E side of Long Loch and join route at road over from Driffenbeg. Save 6km 3.8ml.

76. *Corse Hill.*

Ordnance Survey map 64. Distance from city centre to car parking: 18.8km 11.7ml. Walking distance from parking: 8.5km 5.3ml. Height of climbing: 126m 413f. A walk along a forestry road for a day when the hills are too wet for comfort, to the highest point between Glasgow and the Irvine Valley at Darvel.

Park car at side of road just before Carrot. NS577482. To get there, go via Clarkston, Busby, B767, and Eaglesham. Cross straight over B764 at Eaglesham and at Y junction just after Nether Enoch, go right.

Walk forward and just before Carrot Burn turn left along road which goes between house and lock-up. Go through three gateways. At junction, do not turn left. The road climbs and zig-zags not far from burn. It passes through a small woodland, then enters an area of young forestry. At the top of the road, climb a few metres up to the top of Corse Hill (376m 1233f. TP. BM S1604). Immediately behind the triangulation pillar, there is a building with a dome-like erection on top – this is a radar site for the weather forecasting network. The return is by the same route.

As an alternative return, it is possible to strike SW over rough terrain, alongside forestry, to Quarry Hill (332m 1088f) near High Overmuir farm. From here the old route from Darvel to Eaglesham leads N to Carrot. The O.S. map 71 would also be required for this part. The total walking distance of this route is 12.7km 7.9ml.

It is not practicable to shorten this walk.

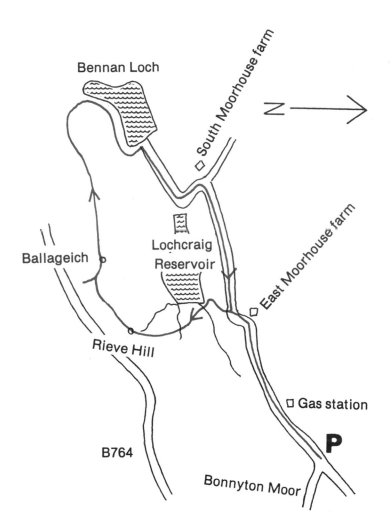

Bennan Loch

South Moorhouse farm

N →

Ballageich

Lochcraig
Reservoir

East Moorhouse farm

Rieve Hill

Gas station

P

B764

Bonnyton Moor

WALK 77

77. *Ballageich Hill.*

Ordnance Survey map 64. Distance from city centre to car parking: 15km 9.3ml. Walking distance from parking: 13.5km 8.4ml. Height of climbing: 105m 344f. This is an easy, short and pleasant country walk, going over a hill which has become well known because of its prominence rather than its height.

Park car on Bonnington Moor road. NS544522. To get there go to Newton Mearns on A77. At the cross turn left to Mearns, then right and left on to Eaglesham road. After 1.8km 1.1ml and just before bends round mound with trees, turn right along road marked 'Bonnyton Golf Club'. After 1.5km 1ml a road from the golf club and B764 joins on the left. Park just past this junction.

Walk along road, passing British Gas station (which reduces the pressure of the gas coming from the mains) to East Moorhouse farm. At the start of farm buildings the road turns left. Continue on it. There is a part which is like a ford, but a row of stones at the side lets walkers cross without getting wet. Shortly after this, cross fence on left on to grass-covered remains of old track. At crest of this track cut to the left across land to the end of Lochcraig Reservoir. Go through a gap in a wall, and then a gap in another wall near a single tree.

Then climb up Rieve Hill and across to Ballageich (335m 1099f) where you will find a path on top. Turn left along to edge above road (B764). Look down the well-worn path from the car parking on road below. Retrace your steps along path walking the whole length of the hill, before descending to S end of Bennan Loch. Walk along E side of loch to join track leading through South Moorhouse farm and East Moorhouse farm to start.

It is not practicable to shorten this walk.

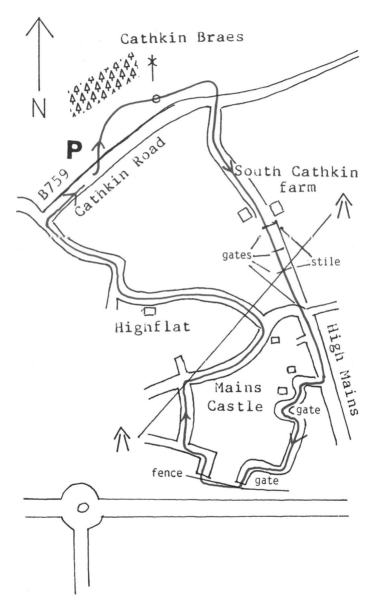

Cathkin Braes

N

P

B759

Cathkin Road

South Cathkin
farm

gates

stile

Highflat

High Mains

Mains
Castle

gate

fence

gate

WALK 78

78.   *Cathkin Braes and Mains Castle.*

Ordnance Survey map 64. Distance from city centre to car parking: 10.2km 6.4ml. Walking distance from parking: 13.1km 8.2ml. Height of climbing: 50m 164f. Since Cathkin Braes is one of the obvious hills seen from the centre of Glasgow, and since the view of Glasgow and the Clyde valley from it is second to none, this walk is included. But it is not a climber's walk, it is a pleasant ramble.

Park car at lay-by on B759 E of Carmunnock. NS610579. To get there, go via King's Park and B766 to Carmunnock. In that village, turn left along 'Cathkin Road'. When the road levels out, park in first lay-by.

Walk on to land on left (N) of road. There are a number of paths. Take one going across to woodland. There is a well-trodden path along in front of that woodland. Follow it to the right. When it divides, fork left but do not drop down to the left. You will come out near the police transmitter mast. Go over to it as it is the summit of Cathkin Braes (192m 630f. TP. BM S3662). You are now in a park owned by the City of Glasgow District Council, and the summit is called 'Queen Mary's Seat' after Mary Queen of Scots. On a clear day the whole city can be seen from this point, and also the Campsies to the N, the Kilpatricks to the NW, and the more distant mountains as a background. The housing scheme immediately below is Castlemilk.

Walk E along the top of the escarpment to indicator. There used to be a flagpole here. Continue and go down path at end of shelter building. Turn right along front of line of trees with children's swings beside them. Watch for gate through fence on right. Go across to and through that gate onto road, crossing over and into facing side road. Soon there is the entrance to 'Cathkin Quarry Landfill Site'. Pass this and for a short distance the walk is marred by the ugliness on the left. However, shortly the road leads through pleasant country, passing cottages on the right and South Cathkin farm on the left. Go straight ahead along track, crossing four gates on the way, two with stiles to make it easy. This takes you to a road, coming from the right and turning into the southerly direction you are going.

Walk down this motor road to second turning on the right. Go along this to High Mains farm, through the farmyard and follow a farm track down to Mains Castle which can now be seen. This castle was owned by John (Red) Comyn whom Robert Bruce killed in the church in Dumfries in 1306. It passed to John Lindsay of Dunrod in 1382. Only the tower remains, but it is kept in excellent condition.

Continue along track, through a gate, alongside various fields, until it reaches a gate at a new motor road. Go through gate, immediately turn right, and walk alongside a fence uphill. At the highest point, cross fence onto the cut-off end of an old country road. This shortly turns left. Then take first road off on right. Follow this to a crossroad below overhead electric lines. Turn right, then first left opposite Rogerton Farm. This road passes Highflat Farm and twists and turns until it reaches Cathkin Road on which you parked your car. Turn right up to this.

It is not practicable to shorten this walk.

Den A'an. Walk 53.

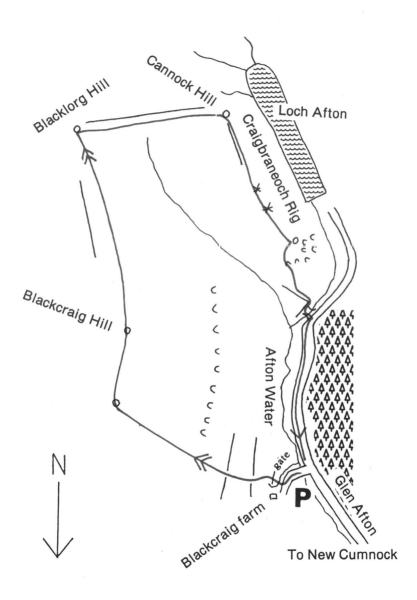

Blacklorg Hill

Cannock Hill

Loch Afton

Craigbraneoch Rig

Blackcraig Hill

Afton Water

N

gate

Blackcraig farm

P

Glen Afton

To New Cumnock

WALK 79

DOON AND AFTON

79. Blackcraig and Blacklorg Hills (Glen Afton).

Ordnance Survey map 77. Distance from city centre to car parking: 72.9km 45.3ml. Walking distance from parking: 16.7km 10.4ml. Height of climbing: 678m 2224f. A fine walk round the four tops above this lovely valley. Early ascent means that most of the walking is on the hill tops.

Park car in Glen Afton at Blackcraig Farm road end. NS631080. To get there take A77 (Glasgow to Kilmarnock), but half way along Kilmarnock bypass turn left along A76. Pass through Mauchline and Cumnock. At the right-angle turn in New Cumnock, take the B741 Dalmellington road, but almost immediately turn left along Glen Afton road. Go along this for 5.5km 3.4ml.

Walk up farm road and, immediately before farm, cross river, go through gate in wall, and turn up hill. Pass through gaps in two walls. Climb steadily towards 675m 2214f point shown on map then along S to rocky and boggy summit of Blackcraig Hill (700m 2298f. TP. BM S5833. Cairn). Continue in same direction descending (keep well to right of fence so that you cross the top of pass between the hills, except in mist when the fence should be followed) and then up Blacklorg Hill (680m 2231f). The boundary line between Strathclyde Region and Dumfries and Galloway Region passes through this top, but otherwise the walk is entirely in the former.

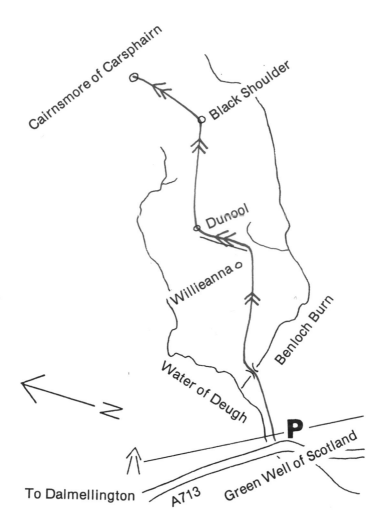

Cairnsmore of Carsphairn

Black Shoulder

Dunool

Willieanna

Benloch Burn

Water of Deugh

P

N

To Dalmellington   A713   Green Well of Scotland

WALK 80

Return along old dyke to Cannock Hill (594m 1948f. Cairn). This is immediately above and looking down onto Loch Afton. Then go down along wall on right and up by cairns over Craigbraneoch Rig to unnamed top (575m 1886f. Cairn). This provides an excellent view. Great care should be taken in descent (in mist, return and descend to burn on E farther back). Go to the E side, slightly back and go down towards burn until you see a grassy slope towards the joining of the waters. Follow this down keeping to left of fence. Follow round fence to bridge across river and then to road. Go along road to start.

To shorten the walk, after descending from Blackcraig Hill, swing round to the right, across burn, and up unnamed top, resuming route. Save 5.6km 3.5ml.

80. Cairnsmore of Carsphairn.

Ordnance Survey map 77. Distance from city centre to car parking: 92.7km 57.6ml. Walking distance from parking: 16.4km 10.2ml. Height of climbing: 624m 2047f. A long car journey. The walk can be quite wet underfoot to start, but once higher it is fine mountain walking. The name 'Cairnsmore' means 'great rocky hill'; and 'Carsphairn' is a combination of 'alder swamp' (Norse), and 'alder tree' (Gaelic). It is a Corbett.

Park car at 'Green Well of Scotland' on A713 (Ayr to Castle Douglas). NX557946. To get there, take A77 (Glasgow to Kilmarnock), bypassing Kilmarnock and Ayr, then on to A713 to about 14km 8.7ml past Dalmellington.

Leave the road on NE side, keeping to SE of river (Water of Deugh). Cross bridge over Benloch Burn, skirt the right (E) side of Willieanna, and follow a dyke to ascend Dunool (536m 1758f). Then make for Black Shoulder (688m 2257f) and by path to the summit of Cairnsmore of Carsphairn (797m 2612f. TP. BM S1597. Two cairns). Return by same route.

It is not practicable to shorten this walk, except by returning before reaching the target.

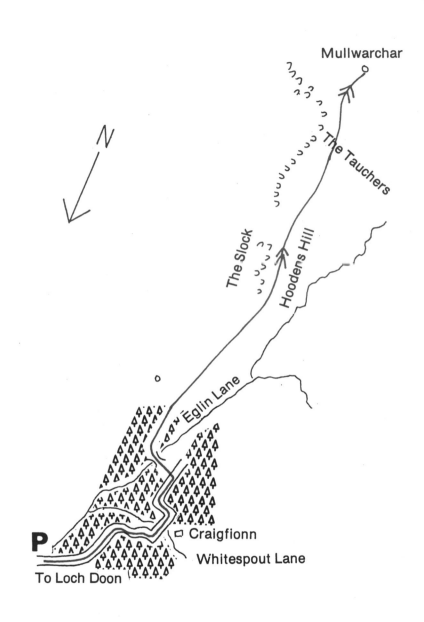

Mullwarchar

The Tauchers

The Slock

Hoodens Hill

Eglin Lane

N

P

Craigfionn

Whitespout Lane

To Loch Doon

WALK 81

81. *Mullwharchar.*

Ordnance Survey map 77. Distance from city centre to car parking: 93.3km 58ml. Walking distance from parking: 27km 16.8ml. Height of climbing: 499m 1637f. A long journey to start and a long walk, but not too much climbing. Can be boggy at parts. The name means 'the hill of the hunting horn'. This countryside has a fascination of its own.

Park car at the end of road along Loch Doon. NX468942. To get there, take A77 (Glasgow to Kilmarnock), bypassing Kilmarnock and Ayr, then on to A713 to about 2.3km 1.4ml past Dalmellington. Turn right along Loch Doon road and follow this road alongside the loch, past Loch Doon Castle (13th century, re-erected in 1935 when the level of the loch was raised), then turning away from the loch to gate into forestry. Park here.

Walk along the road in forest and after 1.45km 1ml (near Craigfionn) turn left down road to Whitespout Lane (a lane is a waterway joining two lochs). Cross this by bridge and shortly thereafter take left fork. Follow this road southwards for 0.75km 0.5ml through the forest, then fork left again through firebreak to take you to and across bridge over Eglin Lane. Turn right alongside this river, then up the ridge of Hoodens Hill (with the face of The Slock to the E). Continue in this direction, past the top of The Tauchers (very deep precipices) and so to the conical summit of Mullwharchar (692m 2270f. Cairn). Return by same route.

It is not practicable to shorten this walk, except by returning before the end.

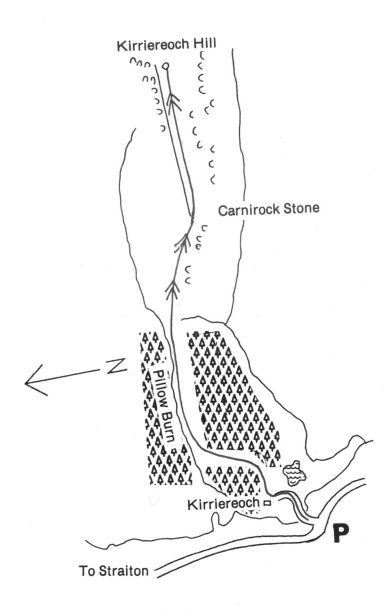

Kirriereoch Hill

Carnirock Stone

N

Pillow Burn

Kirriereoch

P

To Straiton

WALK 82

82. *Kirriereoch Hill.*

Ordnance Survey map 77. Distance from city centre to car parking: 85.4km 53.1ml. Walking distance from parking: 19.5km 12.1ml. Height of climbing: 575m 1886f. A walk along the Strathclyde/Dumfries and Galloway regional boundary climbing to a typical top of this excellent hill-walking area. This hill is known as 'the hill of the great corrie', and is a Corbett.

Park car near Kirriereoch on the Straiton to Bargrennan road. NX360860. To get there take A77 via Kilmarnock and Ayr bypasses, leaving before Maybole along B7045 through Kirkmichael and Straiton (a beautiful village). Kirriereoch road end is reached after a farther 19.5km 12.1ml.

Walk past the hamlet of Kirriereoch and NE through forest break to and alongside Pillow Burn. On emerging from the forest, climb up past Carnirock Stone along rounded ridge with steep rocky slopes on both sides. The remains of a fence and then a dyke follow the route to near the top. At the dyke's highest point, go S for short distance to summit of Kirriereoch Hill (786m 2579f. Cairn). Return by same route.

It is not practicable to shorten this walk, except by turning back before reaching Kirriereoch Hill.

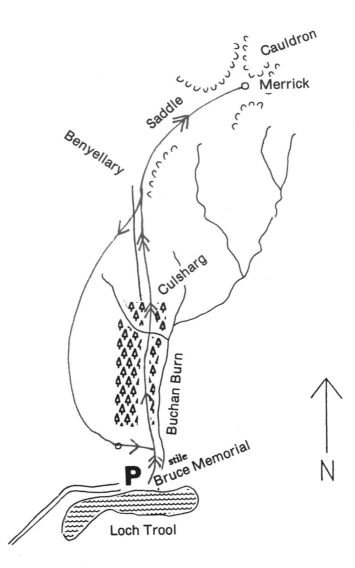

Cauldron

Merrick

Saddle

Benyellary

Culsharg

Buchan Burn

stile
Bruce Memorial

P

Loch Trool

WALK 83

83. Merrick.

Ordnance Survey map 77. Distance from city centre to car parking: 100km 62ml. Walking distance from parking: 18.8km 11.7ml. Height of climbing: 743m 2437f. A long car journey, but a climb very much worth doing in good weather. Is steep in places. It is the highest hill south of the Highlands, and is a Corbett. Together with Tarfessock, Kirriereoch, and Benyellary these mountains are called 'The Range.of the Awful Hand'.

Park car at Loch Trool car park, near Bruce's Stone. This is a monument recording a victory over the English in 1307, and is owned by the National Trust for Scotland. NX514436. To get there take A77 to Girvan and A714 towards Newton Stewart. At Bargrennan turn left up minor road and then right along Glen Trool road. (An alternative and much more interesting, but slower, route is to leave the A77 before Maybole, and go along B7045 through Kirkmichael and Straiton. From here the road is over high ground and reaches the Glen Trool road before Bargrennan.)

Since this is a favourite walk there is a trodden waymarked route. Cross a stile, follow arrow up higher path. This goes along the W side of Buchan Burn through the forest and past the Culsharg bothy. Uphill the path meets a dyke which leads onto Benyellary (719m 2360f. Cairn). It then turns NE and across the Saddle, or Neive of the Spit, up to the summit of Merrick (843m 2765f. TP. BM S1568. Cairn). Avoid the 250m 800f drop on the NE side known as the Cauldron of the Merrick.

Return by the same route to Benyellary, then SW over Bennan to Fell of Eschoncan (360m 1180f). Then descend to the E to join upward path.

To shorten the walk, do not return via Bennan, but as outward route. Save 2.3km 1.4ml.

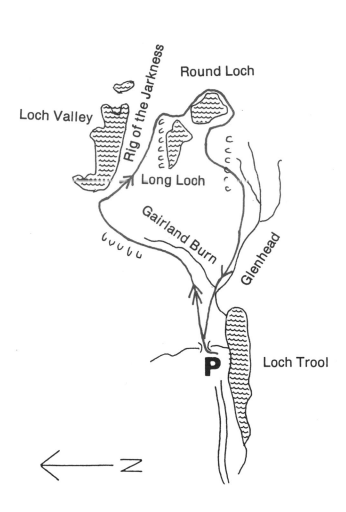

Round Loch

Loch Valley

Rig of the Jarkness

Long Loch

Gairland Burn

Glenhead

Loch Trool

P

N

WALK 84

84.   *Lochs of Glenhead.*

Ordnance Survey map 77. Distance from city centre to car parking: 100km 62ml. Walking distance from parking: 13.2km 8.2ml. Height of climbing: 289m 950f. A shorter walk from Glen Trool among the beautiful scenery of this part of the country.

Park car at Loch Trool car park. NX514436. See walk 83.

Go along road which descends from last car park. Leave this at second notice 'Loch Valley'. Follow path going ENE which joins Gairland Burn and reaches Loch Valley. On a warm day you might get a dip in the refreshing waters. Turn right along S side of loch and cross Rig of the Jarkness to the end of rocks. Descend steeply to Long Loch of Glenhead, then walk round E, S and W sides of Round Loch of Glenhead. Curve back to left, descend steep side of hill and then turn and walk W gradually coming down to Glenhead and so back to car.

To shorten the walk, from Loch Valley return by outward route. Save 4.8km 3ml.

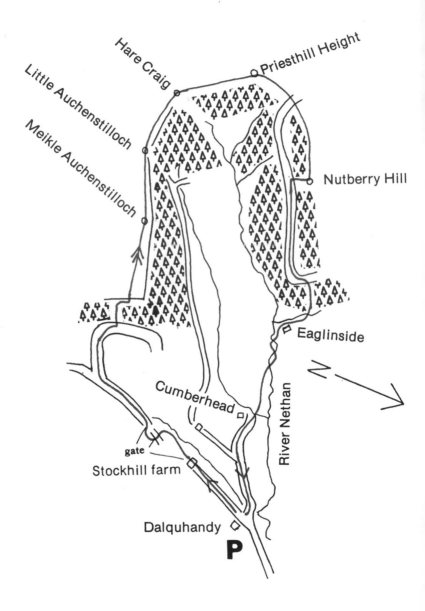

Hare Craig

Priesthill Height

Little Auchenstilloch

Meikle Auchenstilloch

Nutberry Hill

Eaglinside

Cumberhead

River Nethan

gate

Stockhill farm

Dalquhandy

P

WALK 85

CLYDESDALE

85.   *Auchinstilloch and Nutberry Hills.*

Ordnance Survey map 71. Distance from city centre to car parking: 45.4km 28.2ml. Walking distance from parking 22.4km 13.9ml. Height of climbing: 376m 1233f. A mixture of old railway track, forestry roads, heathery moorland and forest breaks, with little climbing. Avoid in misty weather.

Park car at Dalquhandy (about 6.3km 4ml SSW of Lesmahagow). NS788351. To get there go via East Kilbride and Strathaven. Continue on A726 towards Kirkmuirhill, but 5.6km 3.5ml past Strathaven (at Kype Water Bridge) turn right along minor road. This joins a road from Lesmahagow at bridge across Logan Water near Yonderton. Follow sign 'Coalburn' across bridge (the road then turns left) and follow road, which crosses another bridge and turns sharp left, to crossroads. Turn right along road signposted 'Cumberhead' and after 1.3km 0.8ml turn left up farm road marked 'Stockhill'.

Walk along this road through Stockhill farm, and over track, past remains of a building, leading to old railway line. To get on to that line, either go through gate; under bridge, turn right up to track, and through another gate, or, if new open-cast boundary fence is erected, follow it round to the S for a short distance before joining the rail line. Follow rail line for about 1.6km 1ml; then turn right up forestry road. As you ascend you will see on your left the hills in front of

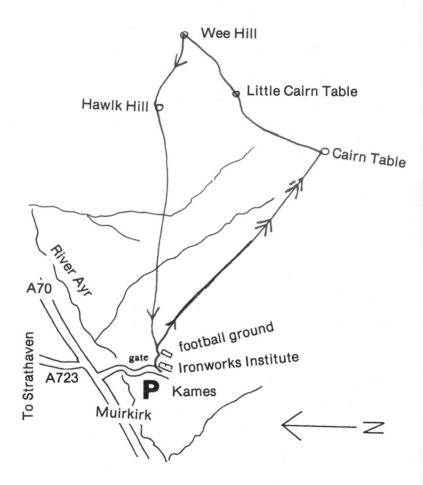

WALK 86

Auchinstilloch, but continue on road to right, with forest on both sides. The road then swings to the left before a sharp bend to the right. At that bend look for firebreak on left. Go up this to end. Turn right along between fence and forest. Near the top, cross the fence, and walk over roughish heathery ground in SW direction, keeping a fence with forestry behind it on your right. Before the top there is a slight downhill, then up to the summit of Meikle Auchinstilloch (491m 1609f).

The fence turns left. Follow it round, over a wood gate, to Little Auchinstilloch. Keep following the fence over rough ground to top of Hare Craig (flat and featureless). Continue NW to Priesthill Height (491m 1615f), passing on your left the start of the Ponesk Burn which is really the source of the River Ayr. Go N down to forestry road, crossing this and on to ridge free of trees and along to Nutberry Hill (522m 1712f. TP. BM S5462). Descend to right of upward route, through firebreak to road, turn left along it and after it turns up left cut through trees to small deepish valley out of woodland. Turn right along this, crossing it, to remains of Eaglinside farm.

Follow pleasant grassy old road over bridges across River Nethan to Cumberhead, and so by road to car.

To shorten the walk, after Hare Craig, go NE down through trees and join forestry road (turn right) and back to start. Save 2.9km 1.8ml.

86. Cairntable.

Ordnance Survey map 71. Distance from city centre to car parking: 49.1km 30.5ml. Walking distance from parking: 13.5km 8.4ml. Height of climbing: 490m 1612f. A clear conical top which invites hill walkers to reach its top. Quite easy.

Park car at Kames, Muirkirk. NS696265. To get there travel to Strathaven (A726 via East Kilbride, or A728 via Hamilton), then A723 to Muirkirk. On arrival at Muirkirk turn right along A70 and almost immediately

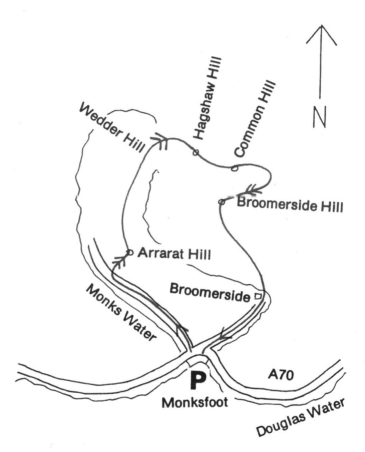

WALK   87

left along road, signposted 'Kames', leading over River Ayr. At fork in road, turn right and go up to building with large clock tower. Park here. This building was originally the Ironworks Institute in which were provided reading rooms and other facilities for the workers in the ironworks and mines. The ironworks were directly opposite the Institute but are now demolished.

Walk back to start of Ironworks Cottages (next to Institute) and turn up track. Go through gate and up to old football ground. Take the route round the left side of this ground and just past it you will notice a concrete fence post. This is the first of a number of such posts which guide you until you reach a path beside a fence. Follow this path. The fence becomes a wall. The path goes right up to the summit of Cairn Table (593m 1945f. TP. BM S1562. Two cairns). The E cairn is the summit, the W cairn is a war memorial.

Leave top in NE direction to Little Cairn Table (516m 1692f), then Wee Hill (434m 1424f). Turn to NW direction and make for Hawlk Hill (390m 1279f). From that top proceed W across to start of walk.

To shorten the walk, return from Cairn Table summit by outward route. Save 3.4km 2.1ml.

87. Arrarat and Hagshaw Hills.

Ordnance Survey map 71. Distance from city centre to car parking: 55.7km 34.6ml. Walking distance from parking: 11.6km 7.2ml. Height of climbing: 285m 938f. A short walk around a few easy-to-walk hills in this interesting area.

Park car at Monksfoot on Douglas to Muirkirk road, NS787285. To get there take M74 and A74 to Douglas Mill and turn right along A70. Pass through Douglas and 2.4km 1.5ml past Glespin park on disused railway station yard on S side of road, between road and short bypass, or thereby at side of newly realigned road.

Walk along old road on right-hand side of Monks Water and after 1.5km 1ml turn right and climb up

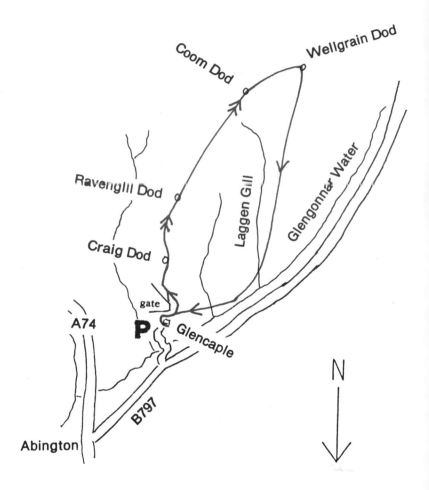

Coom Dod

Wellgrain Dod

Ravengill Dod

Laggen Gill

Glengonnar Water

Craig Dod

gate

A74

P

Glencaple

B797

Abington

N

WALK 88

Arrarat Hill (425m 1394f). Proceed N down hillside, then up Wedder Hill and Hagshaw Hill (474m 1554f). Go WSW across to Common Hill (488m 1601f. TP. BM S6108), then to Broomerside Hill. From here go down SE side of hill to E side of burn to Broomerside, where you can join a road down to Monksfoot and the car.

It is not practicable to shorten this walk.

88. *Wellgrain Dod.*

Ordnance Survey map 71. Distance from city centre to car parking: 63.2km 39.3ml. Walking distance from parking: 12.7km 7.9ml. Height of climbing: 308m 1010f. A gentle hill walk in sheep-rearing country.

Park car at Glencaple near Abington. NS920214. To get there motor along M74 and A74 (Glasgow to Carlisle) and leave by B797 on right at Abington. 1.2km 0.8ml along this road leave on left, down road which crosses Glengonnar Water and goes up to Glencaple (a shepherd's house).

Walk farther up the road then turn right along track beside wall. At gate turn left and follow wall round to left. Strike up ridge to top of Craig Dod (436m 1430f) then on to Ravengill Dod (538m 1756f. TP. BM S6134). Follow this along to second top (550m 1804f), then Coom Dod. Around here you may see a trap for hooded crows, birds which the shepherds detest because they pick out lambs' eyes. Cross over SW to Wellgrain Dod (553m 1814f). There are entrances to old mine workings around here.

Return along same hill farther to the W, down Laggen Gill to Glengonnar Water and round to start.

It is not practicable to shorten this walk.

201

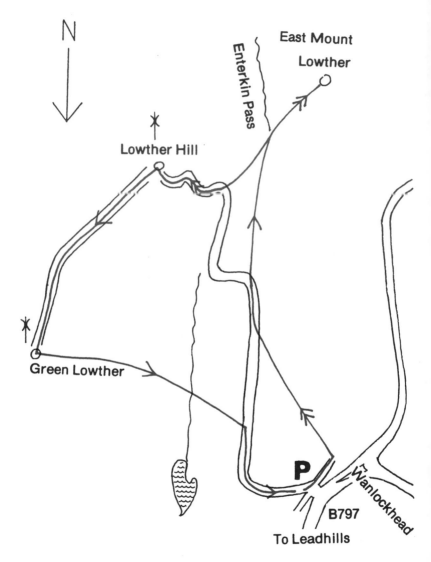

N

East Mount
Lowther

Enterkin Pass

Lowther Hill

Green Lowther

P

Wanlockhead

B797

To Leadhills

WALK 89

89. Lowther Hills.

Ordnance Survey map 71. Distance from city centre to car parking: 73.7km 45.8ml. Walking distance from parking: 14.2km 8.8ml. Height of climbing: 464m 1522f. This mixture of road and rough pathway takes you to the 'top of the world' — a Southern Uplands high-level walk.

Park car at Wanlockhead (the highest village in Scotland) — about 90m 100y up and to the side of the road to Lowther Hill. NS880131. To get there motor along M74 and A74 (Glasgow to Carlisle) and leave by B797 on right at Abington. Pass through Leadhills and just before arriving at Wanlockhead turn left.

This was an area of mining for minerals in past centuries. Gold was extracted from about 1510 to 1620, but latterly lead was the important mineral and it was mined up to 1914. The railway line was opened in 1901-3 and closed in the 1930s.

Find track of old railway line running parallel to B797 and nearer to it than where car is parked. It is now a road running S. Walk along this to Southern Uplands Way notice, and turn left along and up the Way route. When about half way up, when the road swings to the right, but the Way path goes straight on up, go along the road. When the road swings to the left, leave it and make for East Mount Lowther (631m 2069f). (On the way, at the col, look down to the left, i.e. along the Enterkin Pass, which used to be part of the route from Glasgow to Dumfries.) After reaching this top, return to road and follow this up to top of Lowther Hill (724m 2378f) — this is a radar station for airways navigation. Until this point the walk has been in the Dumfries and Galloway Region, but from here it is in Strathclyde Region. Next, walk NE along road to Green Lowther (732m 2403f. TP. BM S6131. Cairn). Here there is a repeater station for television, etc. Leave this summit in a WNW direction down hill, then over burn and up to join road back to car.

To shorten the walk, when you reach the road on the Way route, do not leave it until you arrive at Lowther

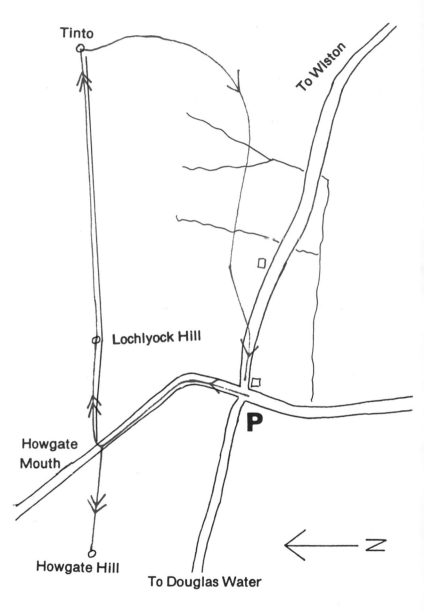

Tinto

To Wiston

Lochlyock Hill

Howgate
Mouth

P

Howgate Hill

To Douglas Water

N

WALK 90

Hill (omitting East Mount Lowther). Continue from there. Save 4.2km 2.6ml.

90.   Howgate Hill and Tinto.

Ordnance Survey map 72. Distance from city centre to car parking: 55.5km 34.5ml. Walking distance from parking: 15.1km 9.4ml. Height of climbing: 516m 1692f. A different way to climb Tinto, avoiding the, sometimes, busy path. Quite easy and very pleasant.

Park car near junction of B7055 (Douglas Water to Wiston) and road going up to Howgate Mouth. NS925331. To get there, take M74 and A74 (Glasgow to Carlisle), and leave on left by A70 (Edinburgh), then on right by B7055.

Walk N along road to Howgate Mouth (a Roman road ran through here). Leave road by climbing Howgate Hill (444m 1456f) on left. Return to road, cross it and, following wall, climb Lochlyock Hill (529m 1734f). This is a favourite hill for hang-gliders enjoying their sport. Continue onto Tinto (707m 2335f. TP.BM S8052. Two cairns), where there was a Druid temple. The hill is also known as Tintock Tap. The massive quantity of stones at the summit is said to have been brought there by local people as penance, on instruction of their priests. However, archeologists generally date this bronze-age cairn as 1000-3000BC.

Return by leaving in SE direction avoiding the very steep face to the S. Then, when below the level of that face, walk round to the W keeping above the cultivated land and trees until past Greenhill farm, when the road should be joined. Walk along road to starting point.

To shorten the walk, omit the climb to Howgate Hill. Save 3.3km 2.1ml.

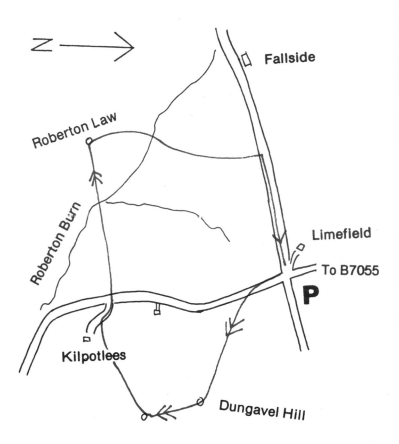

N →

Fallside

Roberton Law

Roberton Burn

Limefield

To B7055

P

Kilpotlees

Dungavel Hill

WALK 91

91.   *Dungavel Hill and Roberton Law*.

Ordnance Survey map 71. Distance from city centre to car parking: 56.8km 35.3ml. Walking distance from parking: 12.1km 7.5ml. Height of climbing: 407m 1339f. This is a short but enjoyable walk to the top of a prominent cone-shaped hill and a contrasting flattish top alongside.

Park car near Limefield at crossroads 3.5km 2.2ml N of Roberton on A73. NS928314. To get there take M74 and A74 (Glasgow to Carlisle), and leave on left by A70 (Edinburgh), then right by B7055. 5km 3.1ml along this road turn right at house, down road to next crossroad. Park near here.

Walk S along road then leave on left side and climb up hill to summit of Dungavel Hill (510m 1673f. TP. BM S6040). Go S down and up other top. This is forested, but there is a forest road through and near the top. Follow this until it is open on lower (right) side. Walk down beside fence and wall to road at Kilpotlees. Turn right along this road. Follow this down and cross motor road. Go W over Roberton Burn (you will have to look for a suitable place) to Roberton Law (377m 1237f). You will notice a broad band of green growth stretching N and S. This covers a gas main pipe. Leave on N side, again crossing Roberton Burn, to road from Fallside. Turn right along to start.

To shorten the walk, after Kilpotlees, instead of crossing motor road, turn right and walk along it to start. Save 4.2km 2.6ml.

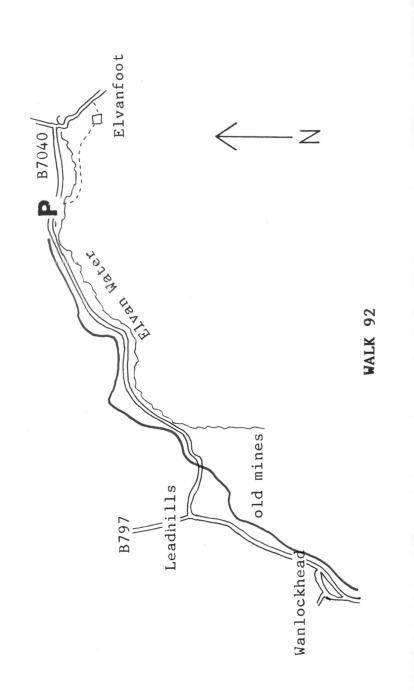

Elvanfoot

B7040

P

Elvan water

B797

Leadhills

old mines

Wanlockhead

N

WALK 92

92. *Elvan Water Valley to Wanlockhead.*

Ordnance Survey map 72 or 78. Distance from city centre to car parking: 71km 44ml. Walking distance from parking: 20.4km 12.7ml. Height of climbing: 160m 520f.

A walk along the valley of the old rail line track (opened in 1901-3 and closed in the 1930s) among hills to the highest village in Scotland.

Park car where the old rail line crosses the B7040 road at NS934176. To get there take M74 (Glasgow to Carlisle) to junction marked 'Thornhill' just past Crawford. Go along the Thornhill road for about 1km, then turn right along B7040. The place to park is about 1½km along this road.

Follow the old rail track which from this point is to the north of the road. Remnants of old mines (gold and lead) can be seen. To the north is Wellgrain Dod and Ravengill Dod, both over 500m high; and to the south is Louise Wood Law which is over 600m high. After 4km/ 2½ml there was a splendid viaduct which took the line over a mountain burn. For safety reasons this had to be demolished. Before it was brought to the ground it was possible for the walker to tread carefully across it, but now it is necessary to climb down the slope and up the other side to rejoin the old track.

The route crosses the road just before Leadhills and skirts round that village before going on to Wanlockhead (the highest village in Scotland). Just before it ends, it is crossed by the Southern Upland Way.

The return journey is by the same route. The only way to shorten the walk is by using a two-car party.

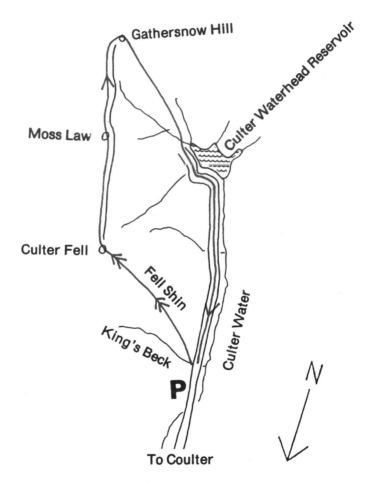

Gathersnow Hill

Culter Waterhead Reservoir

Moss Law

Culter Fell

Fell Shin

King's Beck

Culter Water

P

N

To Coulter

WALK   93

93.   Culter Fell and Gathersnow Hill.

Ordnance Survey map 72. Distance from city centre to car parking: 69.7km 43.3ml. Walking distance from parking: 18.5km 11.5ml. Height of climbing: 726m 2381f. Quite a long, hard walk, but very enjoyable.

Park car in Culter Water road at foot of King's Beck. NT032307. To get there travel via A73 to Lanark and Symington, then A72 (Biggar) and by minor road to A702 when you turn right again to Coulter. When main road turns right at Coulter, go straight on along side road and follow sign 'Birthwood'. After 2.7km 1.7ml take left fork. Then pass Birthwood entrance by keeping to road which turns left then right. Soon you are at King's Beck. There is a small roofless stone building on right of road and a place to park on left.

Climb steeply SE over Fell Shin to Culter Fell (748m. 2455f. TP. BM S5580. Cairn). This is on the Strathclyde/ Borders regional boundary. Following line of fence, descend S by Moss Law to Holm Nick, then climb Gathersnow Hill (690m 2263f). Descend NW to Culter Waterhead Reservoir and go round NE (right) side. Complete the walk by Culter Water to car.

To shorten the walk, from Culter Fell go down by Lang Gill to Culter Waterhead (omitting Moss Law and Gathersnow Hill). Save 7.2km 4.5ml.

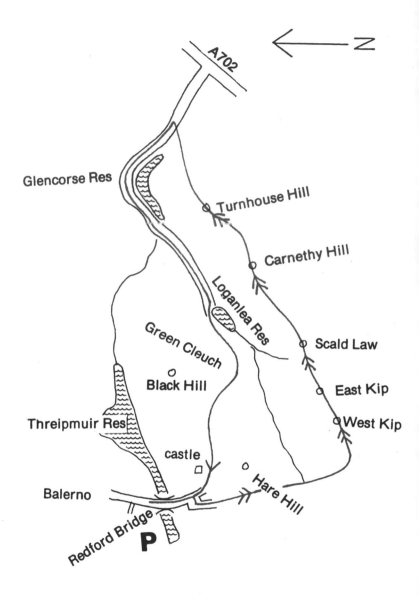

A702

Glencorse Res

Turnhouse Hill

Carnethy Hill

Loganlea Res

Green Cleuch

Black Hill

Scald Law

Threipmuir Res

East Kip

West Kip

castle

Balerno

Hare Hill

Redford Bridge

P

WALK   94

PENTLAND HILLS
AND TWEEDDALE

94.   Scald Law.

Ordnance Survey map 66. Distance from city centre to car parking: 72.1km 44.8ml. Walking distance from parking: 26.5km 16.5ml. Height of climbing: 746m 2447f. This walk covers the main part of the Pentlands in one go, so it is long with a lot of climbing up and down; but these hills are well worth experiencing. It is the only walk in this book in the Lothian Region.

Park car at Redford Bridge. NT165637. To get there, travel E along M8 (Glasgow to Edinburgh) and at Gogar Roundabout at start of Edinburgh turn along 'City Bypass'. Leave at Calder Road and turn W. Then turn left (S) along Riccarton Mains Road and proceed to Currie when you should turn right (W) along A70. Turn left along road to Balerno (Bridge Street), over Water of Leith, turn left along Main Street, Bavelaw Road, Mansfield Road, Cockburn Road to Redford Bridge at Threipmuir Reservoir.

Walk farther along this road in S direction, then turn right, then left, on to path up hills. Path turns E on to the pointed West Kip (550m 1806f), then East Kip, then onto Scald Law (579m 1898f. TP. BM S1573), the highest point in the Pentlands. Continue NE down and up Carnethy Hill (576m 1890f) (there is a 2.4m 8f high cairn on top), down and up Turnhouse Hill (503m

213

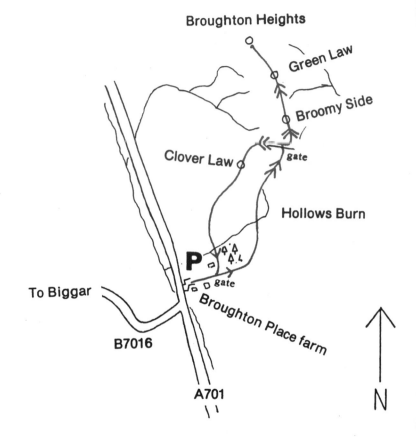

Broughton Heights

Green Law

Broomy Side

gate

Clover Law

Hollows Burn

P

To Biggar

gate

Broughton Place farm

B7016

A701

N

WALK 95

1650f). From here descend to Glencorse Reservoir road. Turn left along this and continue alongside reservoir and on to Loganlea Reservoir. Continue on track which turns right (NW) through the Green Cleuch between Black Hill and Hare Hill and on to start.

To shorten the walk, descend from Scald Law to Green Cleuch (omitting Carnethy Hill and Turnhouse Hill). Save 13.2km 8.2ml.

95.   Broughton Heights.

Ordnance Survey map 72. Distance from city centre to car parking: 71.9km 44.7ml. Walking distance from parking: 12.4km 7.7ml. Height of climbing: 565m 1860f. Excellent walking on rolling grassy tops. If the weather is fine, the views are marvellous. It is a Borders Region walk.

Park car in avenue near Broughton Place Farm. NT113371. To get there go via A8 and A73 to Carluke, Carnwath, turn right along B7016 to Biggar, turn left through village, then right on B7016 to Broughton. Turn left on A701 for very short distance, then turn right up road (sometimes marked 'Broughton Gallery'), round farm buildings and up to end of avenue.

Walk straight on, with castle-shaped building on right, along old drove road passing through gate near house on left, small woodland on left, then fording Hollows Burn. The track then becomes a path up the left side of glen to col between Clover Law and Broomy Side. Pass through gate and turn right up Broomy Side (501m 1643f), along to Green Law (547m 1794f) and Broughton Heights (571m 1873f. TP. BM S5679) — the best view in the Southern Uplands.

Return to col between Broomy Side and Clover Law. Ascend Clover Law (493m 1617f). Go along ridge and drop down before woodland to Hollows Burn. Cross this, go on to road, and right to car.

It is not practicable to shorten this walk, except by turning back before reaching Broughton Heights.

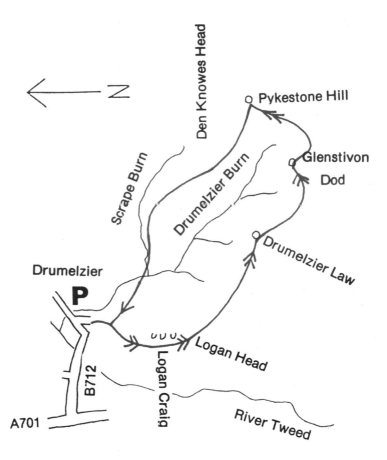

WALK 96

96.   *Pykestone Hill.*

Ordnance Survey map 72. Distance from city centre to car parking: 76.3km 47.4ml. Walking distance from parking: 18km 11.2ml. Height of climbing: 634m 2080f. A fairly easy, but still to be respected, walk on the hills in the Borders Region.

Park car in Drumelzier Burn side road in Drumelzier (pronounced 'Drumeelyer'). NT136339. To get there follow route as for walk 95 to Broughton, then go S along A701 for 2km 1.3ml, and turn left along B712.

Walk S up hill to Logan Craig, then by Logan Head to Drumelzier Law (668m 2192f. Cairn). Descend SE and then up Glenstivon Dod (688m 2257f). Contour round head of Drumelzier Burn and head NE to Pykestone Hill (735m 2414f. TP. BM S6122. Cairn). Return NW by Den Knowes Head, then by road down to the merge of Drumelzier and Scrape Burns. Continue along burn back to start.

To shorten the walk, return from Drumelzier Law by outward route. Save 6.8km 4.2ml.

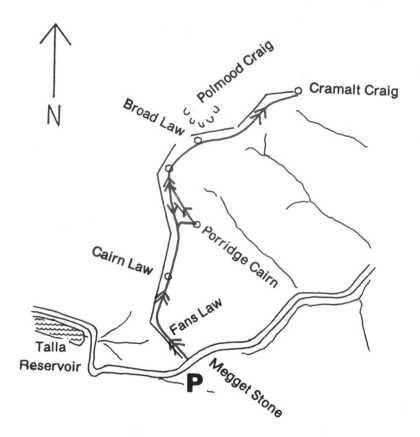

Polmood Craig

Cramalt Craig

Broad Law

Cairn Law

Porridge Cairn

Fans Law

Talla
Reservoir

P

Megget Stone

WALK 97

97. *Broad Law and Cramalt Craig.*

Ordnance Survey map 72. Distance from city centre to car parking: 93.6km 58.2ml. Walking distance from parking: 17.1km 10.6ml. Height of climbing: 703m 2314f. A climb to over 2000 feet and a high-level walk in this gentle hill-walking country in the Borders Region.

Park car on Talla Reservoir — Megget Water road near Megget Stone. NT150203. To get there go via A8 and A73 to Carluke, Carnwath, turn right along B7016 to Biggar, turn left through village, then right on B7016 to Broughton. Then go S along A701 for 13km 8ml, and turn left just past Tweedsmuir Church in valley, and up Talla Reservoir road. Continue up this road, past the reservoir and up steep hill to Megget Stone.

Strike uphill, following fence, in NW direction over Fans Law and on to Cairn Law (717m 2353f). Continue N then turn on to Porridge Cairn (759m 2489f). Reverse a little then on to summit of Broad law (839m 2754f. TP. BM S6127) the second-highest hill in the south of Scotland and a Corbett. There is an aircraft radio beacon here. Proceed round to other top (830m 2723f) above Polmood Craig. Descend to E, following fence, and climb Cramalt Craig (830m 2723f. Cairn) — also a Corbett.

To shorten the walk, return from Broad Law (omitting Cramalt Craig). Save 4.8km 3ml.

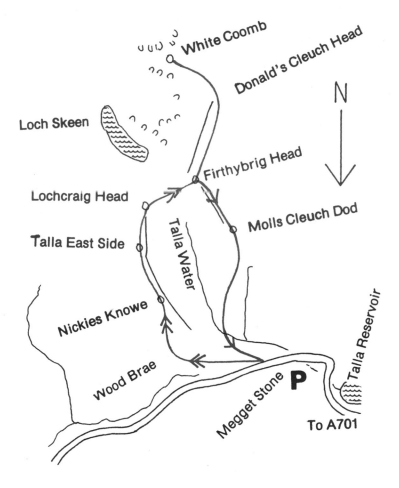

White Coomb

Donald's Cleuch Head

Loch Skeen

Firthybrig Head

Lochcraig Head

Molls Cleuch Dod

Talla East Side

Talla Water

Nickies Knowe

Wood Brae

Megget Stone

Talla Reservoir

To A701

N

WALK 98

98. *White Coomb.*

Ordnance Survey maps 72 and 79. Distance from city centre
to car parking: 93.6km 58.2ml. Walking distance from
parking: 20.4km 12.7ml. Height of climbing: 572m 1876f. A
long journey to start, so pick a good day in summer. An
excellent area for hill walking.

Park car on Talla Reservoir — Megget Water road near
Megget Stone. NT150203. To get there see walk 97.

Strike onto hills in SE direction, up Wood Brae and by
fence to Nickies Knowe, then Talla East Side and Lochcraig
Head. (From this point to Donald's Cleuch Head the route
is along the Borders Region/Dumfries and Galloway
Region boundary.) Descend SW and up Firthybrig Head
(763m 2504f). Go S along side of dyke, over Donald's
Cleuch Head, then SE to White Coomb (821m 2659f.
Cairn), which is a Corbett. Return to Firthybrig Head then,
following dyke, head NW over Molls Cleuch Dod and down
to start.

To shorten the walk, turn at Firthybrig Head (omitting
Donald's Cleuch Head and White Coomb). Save 8.5km
5.3ml.

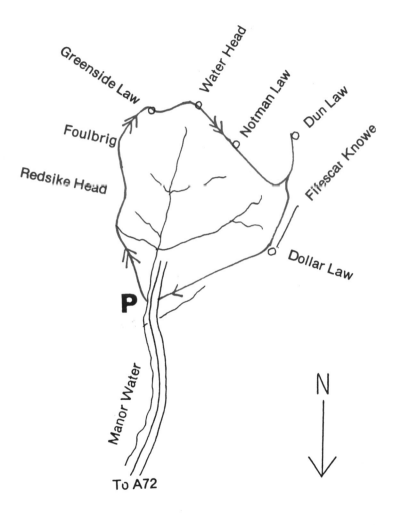

Greenside Law

Water Head

Notman Law

Dun Law

Foulbrig

Fifescar Knowe

Redsike Head

Dollar Law

P

Manor Water

N

To A72

WALK   99

99.   Dun Law.

Ordnance Survey maps 72 and 73. Distance from city centre to car parking: 85km 52.8ml. Walking distance from parking: 15.3km 9.5ml. Height of climbing: 621m 2043f. A six-top round of mountains in the Borders Region.

Park car at head of Manor Water valley. NT199287. To get there go via A8 and A73 to Carluke, A721 to Carnwath, then Elsrickle, and A72 to shortly before Peebles. At this point the road forms a left-turning semi-circle round hills above Edston. Just round the bend there is a road off on the right, cutting back and over the River Tweed where it is joined by Manor Water. Go down this road, and keep right. Do not follow a road over river. At this point turn right, then left. Continue for 9.2km 5.7ml to just below Sting Ring.

Cross Manor Water and walk up track on hill in a SSW direction, round Redsike Head. At Foulbrig strike right up Greenside Law (643m 2111f), then across to Water Head (613m 2012f). Now go NW to Notman Law (734m 2409f). Continue in same direction but when on next ridge turn left and walk along to Dun Law (788m 2585f).

Return along fine level ridge, but straight to Fifescar Knowe (808m 2650f) and, following wall, to Dollar Law (817m 2681f. TP). From that top descend steeply ENE to start.

To shorten the walk, go direct from Notman Law to Fifescar Knowe (omitting Dun Law). Save 1.3km 0.8ml.

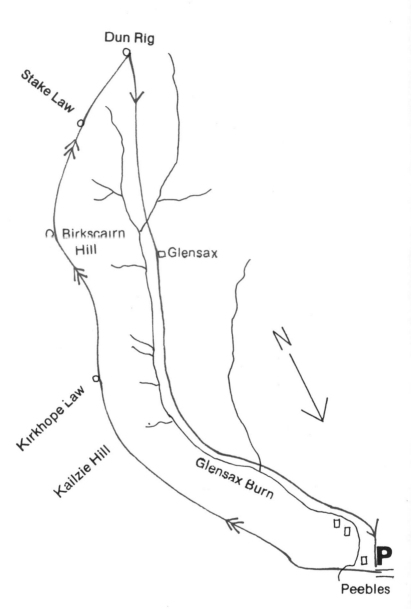

Dun Rig

Stake Law

Birkscairn Hill

Glensax

Kirkhope Law

Kailzie Hill

Glensax Burn

P

Peebles

WALK 100

100. Dun Rig.

Ordnance Survey map 73. Distance from city centre to car parking: 79.5km 49.4ml. Walking distance from parking: 27.7km 17.2ml. Height of climbing 706m 2316f. A long distance to travel, and a long walk — so do it in summer. Well worth doing to see a new area in the Borders Region.

Park car at entrance to Glensax estate in Peebles. NT260393. To get there go via Carluke and Carnwath (see walk 95), and then A721 and A72 to Peebles. On entering Peebles, do not turn up main street. Go over bridge crossing River Tweed. This road turns left and almost immediately there is a road to the right (Springhill Road). Follow this uphill to entrance to estate.

Strike up hill in SE direction along path (being an old drove road which is a right-of-way through to Yarrow as signposted), past Kailzie Hill, over Kirkhope Law (536m 1758f), Birkscairn Hill (662m 2169f) and Stake Law (679m 2229f) to Dun Rig (743m 2433f. TP. BM S1571). Return by NNE descending into valley at Glensax, and joining path along Glensax Burn to start.

To shorten the walk, after Birkscairn Hill go down track to Glensax (omitting Stake law and Dun Rig). Save 6.4km 4ml.

AUTHOR'S COMMENTS AND HINTS

GETTING TO THE START

The hill walks described in this book are based on the
assumption that the walkers have the use of a car. Public
transport is now quite inadequate. The cost of running a
car for the relatively short distances is low when divided
among the members of a party — much less than
spending a whole day motoring. Some groups divide the
cost of petrol used among those travelling in a car, while
others take turns in providing the car. The former has
the advantage that it provides, without any sense of
obligation, for those who do not have a car or are not
keen on driving.

An indication of suitable parking is given in each walk
described. Be sure to avoid obstructing side roads or
gates into fields. Leave space for heavy milk lorries,
tractors, etc. to pass. But do not park on soft ground — it
may be extremely difficult to get the car out when you
return to it at the end of the day. If there is a house or
farm nearby, advise the residents that you are leaving
the car, in order that they will not be worried and
perhaps inform the police.

Do not leave any loose objects on the seats or floor of
the car — put them in the boot. Do not leave wallets or
valuables even in the boot — take them with you.
Unfortunately, a few car parks have been invaded by car
thieves. Check before closing up the car that the keys are

in your possession and not in the car. A spare set handed to another member of the party is a good protection.

While the driver will not want to wear his boots for the journey, the others might do so if the boots are clean, and this will save the trouble of changing footwear at the start.

ACTION AND ATTITUDE

Hill walking is an acquired taste. Some get the habit when very young by being taken by their parents. Others learn to like it later. Many people never get the habit — even if they try. They cannot see the pleasure in putting on heavy boots, carrying a big rucksack, tramping over rough ground, accepting rain and even snow without running for shelter. But for the many who persevere and are bitten by the bug it becomes an essential part of life.

Regularity is important. For someone who is working, is only free at the week-ends, and has other social commitments, then once a month may be all that is possible. For retired persons and others, once a week is desirable. In any case it should at first be an obligation and it will gradually grow into a necessity — a delightful necessity, with pleasure when on the hills and satisfaction and good health thereafter.

While perseverance is part of the hill walker's attitude, never extend yourself beyond your capabilities. Do not go faster than is comfortable. Do not take risks. Do not be afraid to declare that you are tired or out of breath. Everyone feels like that at some time. However, it does pay a walker to acquire a steady pace with few stops.

Ideally one foot should be on firm ground before the other leaves the ground, and one should try to achieve this. But loose stones, slippery grass, ruts covered by heather can result in unsteadiness or even a fall. Good boots can, in such a case, save ankles from injury. Slight discomfort after such a fall will usually quickly disappear after walking for a minute or two.

CLOTHING

The choice of some garments may vary from person to person, but there are essential items if any enjoyment at all is to be had. The following notes illustrate this point:

Footwear — Boots with a solid, thick and gripping sole are essential. The uppers are usually of hard leather with tongue sewn up each side to prevent water penetration. Usually the uppers are sewn to the sole, but sometimes they are bonded. Fully waterproof boots are desirable, but seldom realized. Protection by waxing is advocated by some and condemned by others — it can help to keep water out but it can also rot stitching. After a day's soaking, stuff crumpled newspaper inside to absorb damp and maintain the shape.

Socks and stockings — Wear two pairs of thick wool socks or stockings — first a long pair up over the knee, second a short pair to fold over the top of the boots. Wear these when trying on boots for size.

Gaiters — For cold or wet days, gaiters are valuable. Nylon is preferred to canvas. The under-boot cords are unnecessary and should be removed.

Breeches or trousers — A pair of breeches or an old pair of trousers are equally suitable, provided they are strong and have good pockets (preferably with zip closures). They should not be tight-fitting.

Overtrousers — For very wet conditions, overtrousers with half length zip side openings are desirable.

Underwear — For winter, good thermal vest and pants are desirable, or two of each. In other seasons, it is a case of personal preference.

Shirt or blouse — A lightweight shirt or blouse of absorbent material with a breast pocket, open neck, and fold-over collar is desirable. The pocket for carrying an odd piece of equipment (compass, pedometer, etc.), the collar to catch the cord of a map case.

Pullover — A wool jumper should be taken along or worn. It provides warmth at higher altitudes, and, under a waterproof jacket, is a good absorber of perspiration.

Jacket — The purposes of the top garment are to retain

the body heat, to stop cold winds penetrating, and to keep out the rain or snow. (Some people prefer two garments — one for warmth and a smock — over the head — for protection from rain). The jacket should be closed by means of zip fasteners and Velcro strips, should have good pockets with zip openings and flaps, and should have a hood tightened by a cord with cord grip.

Hat — A bare head or small wool hat is the choice for general wear, and a Balaclava covering ears and chin for very cold weather. In summer, a sunhat for those who suffer from sunstroke.

Gloves — Wool gloves with waterproof mitts provide warmth and protection. Since the mitts can be used when gripping all sorts of rough items (trees, rocks) they should be hard-wearing.

KIT

Travel light if you can but some kit is essential, especially in our climate and when you leave the roads and go into the hills.

Rucksack — The best way to carry what you must is in a light rucksack — not the large frame variety. Two side pockets are valuable — one for a vacuum flask and one for items hopefully not needed, such as first-aid, wallet, torch, etc. Do not rely on the rucksack being water proof, so contain these items in a plastic bag. If the cord round the opening does not have a cord grip, fit one yourself — in cold weather it is much easier to open and close. The shoulder straps should be adjusted so they won't slide off the shoulders of a nylon jacket — if necessary fix a cord round both of them, at the top, to draw them together.

Map — Always have a suitable map of the area you are covering — an Ordnance Survey 1:50,000 Landranger Series is recommended. For wet weather, carry it in a transparent map case slung round your neck and below the top layer of clothing. Study how to find a National Grid Reference.

Compass — You should always carry a compass. Mists can come down when least expected. Learn how to use a compass.

Whistle — Hopefully you will never need this, but in an emergency it could save your life by indicating your location.

First aid — Plasters, bandages, aspirins, cotton wool (to protect ears from biting winds), salted peanuts (to relieve cramp), and insect repellent (for midges) are all items which you should consider carrying.

Torch — Especially in winter, one can be delayed in the hills until after dark. This situation should be avoided, but if it is not, a torch is most valuable.

Food and drink — Some walkers like a good packed lunch for midday break, others eat little. It is advisable to have some sustenance. Carry it in a plastic box. Liquid refreshment could be tea, coffee, soft drink, etc. Boiling water in a vacuum flask, with tea bags carried separately, allows of a fresh cup of tea when required.

Spectacle case — If you wear spectables, carry a case so that in mist, rain, or snow you can remove your glasses in order to see your way.

Ground seat — At lunch break you will want to sit. You can, of course, sit on a waterproof garment, or you can get a small slightly padded square specially made for the purpose which has a reflecting side to make use of the body heat.

Car keys — Always check before starting out on the walk that the car keys are carried in a secure pocket.

Wallet — Don't leave your wallet in the car. Put it in a waterproof cover and pack in rucksack pocket.

Pedometer — Few people will want to carry a pedometer, but if you do you should clip it in the breast pocket of shirt or blouse, and tie with cord to belt on trousers in case it slips out of pocket.

Walking stick — Some walkers find it helpful, especially in climbing up hills, to have a walking stick. If you do start taking one, try to have your name and address attached to it, since it is very easy to lay down and walk away without it.

Barbed-wire cover — Take a wad of newspaper, a piece of sacking, or a slit length of hose, so that it can be laid over barbed wire of a fence which must be crossed.

Crampons and ice-axe – These are for use in icy conditions which should be avoided except under experienced supervision.

COMPANIONS

While a walk on the hills on one's own can be very enjoyable — solitude is, after all, one of the attractions of the open spaces — most walkers find company an added pleasure. Conversation when on a road or having a bite of food, or even snatches of talk when striding over the heather can be most satisfying.

Probably there should be three or four friends on an outing. Three provides a safeguard should a mishap occur. The victim with, say, a sprained ankle cannot move, the second can go for help, while the third stays with the injured party. More than four becomes a 'trip' with the need for a leader to make the route decisions. These larger parties should confine themselves to walks with an established car park and route.

Above all, go with persons with whom you can relax — companions, becoming friends. It does not matter whether they be male or female — mixed parties can be very successful.

There is the question of stamina. It is no use trying to maintain a group where one is willing and anxious to climb all the Munros in sight, while another is physically unable to do more than a flattish walk. There will always be variations (even within one person's own ability) but these should not be too great.

WEATHER

The only certain comment which can be made about weather in the Glasgow area is that it is never possible, hour by hour, to say with certainty what it will be like. It can change from hot to cold, wet to dry, be exactly the opposite of the weather forecast, and it can change back and forth during one day. The message is, therefore, to prepare for the lot, and hope for the best.

When it is mild in the city, it can be very cold a thousand feet up a hill. On the other hand, when the valleys are full of mist, the sun can shine with brilliance on the mountain tops.

If you go out walking on a regular basis, don't be put off by the weather. It can often turn out much better than it is early in the day. Apart from that, if properly protected, walking in any weather is a great enjoyment.

It is seldom that the weather is so bad that it is not possible to stop for a bite, sheltered from the rain or wind. In summer, if the sun is strong and warm, some people have to protect their head and skin; but at a higher altitude this is unlikely. In winter snows with a strong sun, however, protection is much more likely to be necessary, and dark goggles should be carried. Beware of mists — learn how to deal with them. Keep checking your compass bearings. Remember that mists greatly distort the appearance of distance and size; keep the party together. Heavy rain can quickly cause burns to be in spate and sometimes dangerous to cross. Unless you know of a bridge, go upstream until it is safe to go over.

Overcast skies can bring early darkness. It is always advisable to be back on a well-defined path or road before the sun sets, but if you are caught out use a torch, keep the party together, use your compass, and tread warily.

In a lightning storm, avoid standing on a peak, near a tree, or at the entrance to a cave. It is better to be flat on the ground than to stand up in an open flat area.

Keep a dry set of essential clothes in the car, so that if completely soaked a change is available in order to make the return car journey comfortable. It is not good for the health to travel in wet clothes, and this can apply also to perspiration. A rub down and a change of underwear can work wonders.

SAFETY

The walks described in this book are not dangerous. There are no rock climbs, 'bad steps', or raging torrents to cross. Nevertheless, mishaps can occur on the hills and sometimes with very serious effect. So it is advisable to take precautions.

1. Don't go when unwell.
2. Always have the proper clothing and kit.
3. Have a first-aid kit, and a whistle and torch.
4. Have food and drink. Warm drink unless the weather is very hot.
5. Don't attempt more than you can manage.
6. Don't go faster, to keep up with the others, if it is causing distress.
7. Don't attempt to cross a fast-flowing burn unless you can have secure footholds.
8. Don't walk over brittle rock, wet rock, or icy rock.
9. Only descend a steep slope if you are sure there are secure holds all the way down and a levelling out within a short distance should you slip.
10. Keep in touch with your companions, especially where there is mist.

Probably the most dangerous part of your outing is when you are travelling in the car. So, take care on the road.

RIGHTS AND RESPONSIBILITIES

More correctly, it should be the other way round. Hill walkers have the responsibility of ensuring that they do nothing to harm the land and all that is on it. Always close gates, if you have opened them. Never walk on growing crops. Do not disturb farm animals or game (never take a dog with you). Respect walls and fences, even though the latter sometimes tear your clothes. Never leave litter, watching particularly when you stop for a meal. Do not light fires. Maintain the quiet of the countryside. Avoid sheep grazing land during the lambing season (in the Spring but varying with altitude), grouse moors (12th August to 10th December), and deer country during stalking, which mainly takes place from mid-August to mid-October, but which is permitted from 1st July to 15th February.

If you intend to park your car on, or walk through, private cultivated land, ask permission where this is feasible. Not only does the farmer or other local resident appreciate your doing so, but very often they give you good advice as to your route.

It is sometimes thought that in Scotland there is no law of trespass. This is not so. It is still possible to trespass but you cannot be prosecuted for doing so. However, you can be sued for damage, and you can be asked to leave private ground. If so asked (and this happens very seldom), do so without question (unless you feel very strongly on the question of the freedom to roam on Scottish hills, and are prepared to face the consequences). We are fortunate that we have so many hills, almost all of which we are allowed to walk over freely. While this is what it should be, we must always remember our responsibilities to the countryside. 'Rights of Way' are routes, through private property, over which the public have the right of passage. These are often marked as such. The Scottish Rights of Way Society Ltd. does much to protect these, and deserves support from every hill walker. The best way to do this is to join and pay the very modest membership fee.

INDEX OF PLACES